A Garden of Poets

A Garden of Poets

Poetry Writing in the Elementary Classroom

Mary Kenner Glover
Awakening Seed School, Tempe, Arizona

National Council of Teachers of English
1111 W. Kenyon Road, Urbana, Illinois 61801-1096

Staff Editor: Kurt Austin
Interior Design: Doug Burnett
Cover Design: Pat Mayer
Permissions: Kim Black

NCTE Stock Number: 18232-3050

Library of Congress Cataloging-in-Publication Data

Glover, Mary Kenner.
    A garden of poets: poetry writing in the elementary classroom/
Mary Kenner Glover.
        p.   cm.
    Includes bibliographical references (p.   ).
    ISBN 0-8141-1823-2 (pbk.)
    1. Poetry—Study and teaching (Elementary) 2. Poetry—
Authorship—Study and teaching (Elementary) I. Title.
LB1576.G476 1999
372.62'3—dc21   98-51184
                                                                            CIP

for Bill, with all my heart

Contents

Foreword

In this fine book for teachers, Mary Kenner Glover is simultaneously idealistic and practical. That is, of course, what we want in all our textbooks, but it is rarely achieved. She reveals how it is possible to make educational idealism pragmatic. Each page documents her educational philosophy, revealing—not preaching—her ideas on how children learn.

Mary Glover takes chances. Each chapter begins with her pupils creating a garden. This approach worried me. Would this book be filled like so many others with romantic, feel-good—even arrogant—blather wherein teachers are always successful and never believable, students forever cute and never likable?

No. Mary Glover's garden works. She listens to her students with respect, and they respond with diversity, intelligence, and wisdom. Her listening makes them listen to themselves. They instruct themselves, each other, Mary Glover, and this hoary old writer. She allows her students to learn, then documents their learning and puts it in context so they can carry it with them for the rest of their lives.

Mary Glover connects garden learning with the writing of poetry. This is not ethereal poetry piled so high with the peacock display of adjectives and adverbs that meaning—if it exists—is hidden. The poetry in this book rises out of the earth as do the plants, out of working the earth as do poets.

I must confess I have a prejudice against most student poems. They are wonderful in the context of the class, but they do not travel well. Mary Glover's students' poems travel well. They are connected to experience; they distill experience into truth as good poems do.

Mary Glover also writes with her students and for us. She is an excellent writer, practicing what we all preach in teaching writing. That should not be news, but it is. Many textbooks of how to teach writing are pompous, arrogant, egomaniacally complex, written to impress rather than communicate. Mary Glover's writing is deceptively simple—graceful, clear, wise. She demonstrates effective writing on every page.

In each line of the book she displays and demonstrates the attitudes of the teachers who are able to draw learning out of their students. They not only write poetry, they learn to observe, collect, examine, connect, evaluate, to think.

The book is written for elementary school teachers, but this seventy-three-year-old apprentice poet was taught lesson after lesson by Mary Glover's students and by Mary Glover herself. Yes, I know she quotes me in the book, but that is what writers—student writers and publishing writers—do: they teach each other what they know and didn't know they knew or had forgotten they knew.

A Garden of Poets is a wise and wonderful book that is grounded in the craft that produces poetry. It is written with respect for students and teachers by an expert teacher who puts herself on the line. It is a tough, demanding, challenging book appropriate to the art of poetry, which is a tough, demanding, challenging craft. It is a book that will be read and re-read, a continuous companion to the elementary school language arts teacher. It is also a book that will stand on a shelf near my writing desk to inspire and instruct me so that when I look into the woods outside my office I will find poems emerging from the trees.

—Donald M. Murray

Acknowledgments

A book, like a poem, can sprout from any situation. This one began on a July evening as I walked the wooded Massachusetts neighborhood near my friend Bobbi Fisher's home. Far from my own desert home, we talked about our work as teachers and writers. During this conversation Bobbi suggested the idea of writing a book about poetry. Although I had plans to write a completely different book, I found myself saying, "I *could* write a book about poetry." The rest is history. I am grateful to Bobbi for planting the first seed of *A Garden of Poets*, as well as for being an honest and compassionate friend.

The book quickly received inspiration from two other sources. After my visit with Bobbi, I spent several days of solitude at my friend Annie's writer's cottage in Maine. There, as I wrote the first pages, I rediscovered my love for the writer's life. Thanks to Annie for the gift of those precious days. Later that same summer I was invited to give a keynote address at Hamline University in St. Paul, Minnesota. As I spoke about poetry, shared my students' work, and listened to lines written by teachers like myself, I was overwhelmed by the response I received from Georgia Loughren and the amazing people who surround her. The day reminded me how powerful teachers' stories are and inspired me to continue writing about my own.

There are many to thank for their contributions to my life, who have been my teachers and enabled this book to grow. My parents were my first teachers and continue to support me in my life work. My brother Mick and sister Jane have been consistently generous over the years, especially with their humor. My youngest brother Pat (who is also very funny and was put out that he wasn't mentioned enough in the last book), has always been a responsive reader of my poetry and other writing. In addition, my grandmother Pauline, at ninety-six, continues to encourage my literary self as she has done my whole life.

I am deeply indebted to my spiritual friend and mentor Erma Pounds for her profound guidance with matters of the heart. Knowing Erma has allowed me to arise each morning and face the day with courage, knowing that the road is long and there will be many who need my help along the way. Another traveler of this path, my dear friend Ken Bacher, opened the door to poetry a long time ago and invited me to become a poet through the example of his own writer's life. Ken was the first real poet I knew, and he has remained a steadfast inspiration.

Without the children, parents, and staff at Awakening Seed School, this book would never have come into being. In particular, the children who grew with me as poets in the garden were invaluable teachers as well as creative, fascinating students. They have led me to places as a teacher that I never would have discovered on my own. Supporting my work with these children were two incredible people—Mona Rothenberg, my classroom assistant, who values our daily practice of silent writing as much as I do, and Jan Stanley-Muchow, my friend and colleague who, in addition to numerous other tasks around the school, took field notes and helped me process our garden work with her intuitive and perceptive mind. Both Mona and Jan helped to elevate the work far beyond where it would have been without them.

My work as a teacher and poet has been significantly shaped by my long-standing relationships with Linda Sheppard, Maryann Eeds, and Ralph Peterson. All three have helped to make poetry of my life through our years of conversation and community. Ralph, especially, has taught me to appreciate the value of learning in a community and to push the edges of my thinking at all times. I consider myself fortunate to have such wise colleagues who are, at the same time, loyal and encouraging friends.

I have had the good fortune of knowing several writers who have influenced how I write and live my life as a writer. Don Murray, Ralph Fletcher, Georgia Heard, Susan Stires, Vivian Paley, and Shelley Harwayne have all helped me believe in myself as a writer in ways that wouldn't have happened otherwise. Even though we've spent a relatively short amount of time together physically, they are all with me each time I sit down to write, helping to guide the direction of my work. I am particularly grateful to Don Murray for giving so much to a whole generation of writers (myself included) who have been blessed to know and learn from him.

To Karen Smith, Michael Greer, Pete Feely, and Kurt Austin at NCTE I offer my thanks for their assistance at the various production stages of the book. Karen continues to promote my work in ways that are far-reaching, as she has done for many years. Michael has become a compassionate advocate of my work, and it's encouraging to know there are people in the world like him who make the time to understand. Pete and Kurt have both provided patience and wonderful insights throughout the book's entire process and have made it a better book through their contributions.

On a more personal note, I want to thank my friends Jennifer and Ross Robb for their continued participation in my life as a teacher, writer, and artist. Our life together as friends has been the source of much of the inspiration for my poetry in the past several years, especially the short time I had with their daughter Caitlin. Their friendship has opened up many opportunities for me, and for this I am daily appreciative.

Finally, I offer gratitude to Edith and Roy Glover, my mother- and father-in-law, and to my immediate family—my daughters Sarah and Astraea and my husband Bill. To Sarah I am grateful for inspiring my creativity and for her lifelong spirit of adventure. I am especially thankful to Sarah and her husband Geoff for giving me one of the greatest gifts of my life, little Zoë, the island baby. To Astraea, herself a poet and aspiring young teacher, I give thanks for being a thoughtful, caring friend, as well as a daughter. Future generations of children will be fortunate to call her their teacher. Lastly, I extend my deepest love and appreciation to my husband Bill for making my life work his own, so that all of the young poets and learners who come our way will have a school in which to grow that will make a substantial difference in their lives.

Poems

It floats by to get its love
It gets its love and comes floating
Back with it
Can you guess what it is?

It's paper and pencil

Something else comes floating past
It whispers to the pencil
Please write me down
Write me down on that paper
You found

The thing that went by
Came floating out of my head
It was a poem
It was a lovely poem

It was this poem

—Indra, age 8

Permissions

Introduction

This book caught me by surprise, just as the poetry I write often does as I move through my daily life. I'd never really thought of writing a whole book about poetry, although it has been suggested before. In many respects, the book wrote itself. I am simply the recorder for what has been observed and experienced—like a poet who writes, offering another lens for viewing the world.

Contained in these pages are two stories that at first seemed unrelated. One is about the poetry writing in my classroom. The other describes glimpses of a year of work and play our class was involved in on a small plot of land adjacent to our school building. As I began thinking of one aspect of our school year, the other always seemed to be right there beside it. In trying to write about our work as poets, I found that I also had to write about our work outside. What I realized is that the outdoor work became a strong metaphor for how we live and learn, the greatest lesson in poetry any of us could ever have been given. It caught us by surprise, as all good poetry does, and showed us a new way to see. It helped give us vision and discover the natural poets already residing within each of us.

As the idea for the book evolved, I realized that it is important for teachers to have a book like this one; a book written by another classroom teacher who hasn't had the benefit of extensive specialized training as a poet or as a poetry teacher. I wanted teachers to see how it is possible to include poetry in their classrooms in more than a superficial way and perhaps offer a few suggestions and possibilities for how to do it.

Following prescriptions spelled out by others has never been one of my strengths as a teacher or writer. I have received the most benefit from teachers who have told their stories, given a wealth of suggestions from their own experiences, and then stepped aside, offering an invitation to try whatever seems to make sense. These teachers have encouraged me to develop teaching practices inspired from intuition, and to allow my work as a teacher to be informed by what my students say and do. I am particularly indebted to Donald Murray, Georgia Heard, and Ralph Fletcher—all writers who have significantly shaped my work as a poet and teacher of poetry writing. Their influences as writing teachers will be examined more closely in Chapter 2.

My resistance to following prescribed practices is matched by a related reticence about writing a step-by-step manual on how to teach poetry. Just as I have appreciated the latitude allowed by the teaching and writing styles of my teachers, I want to give the same to others. What I have learned in my two decades of teaching and writing is how to pay attention to children and tell the stories of our work together. I approach this book about poetry in that spirit. It is my hope in telling my story—as a poet and teacher of young poets—that other teachers will find courage, and maybe a bit of inspiration, to risk bringing poetry into their lives. It has been my experience that hearing the stories of other teachers opens up a way to see how I can create my own. Although direct techniques are absolutely necessary at times, there is also value in a more open-ended experience, where we can fill in the gaps ourselves. In many respects, this is how poetry operates. Brief descriptions and fragments of imagery are on the page, leaving spaces for the reader to fill in his or her own meanings.

Working with young poets presents numerous challenges. The poet Rainer Maria Rilke writes, "Ah! but verses amount to so little when one writes them young. One ought to wait and gather sense and sweetness a whole life long . . . and then quite at the end, one might perhaps be able to write ten lines that were good" (1949, 26). Young children who write poetry haven't lived long and rich lives. They are just beginning their life experiences. They often see the world literally and have yet to understand about symbolism and metaphor. They require direct experiences for what they must come to know indirectly. Young writers are sometimes in a hurry and need encouragement to slow down for details. Once their words are on the page they hesitate to revise. Others are so concerned about writing the perfect words in their notebooks that they sit for days during their writing period staring at a blank page. Young writers are tough and delicate at the same time.

Yet they have poetry inside them which offers a life perspective that most adults can't even begin to express. Their words cut to the heart of situations in a way that is unique to a child. The wisdom and insights of their poems force us to pause and remember that these young poets are our teachers at the same time as we are theirs.

Keeping that in mind, this book about teaching poetry to young children is also about using poetry and poetic experiences to learn from children. It is a reflection on work that has been informative over many years, and one year in particular that produced a metaphor for thinking more deeply about the responsibilities of teaching poetry to young children. In sharing this work with other teachers, it is my hope that it will not only provide ideas for teaching poetry but also open up new ways to reflect on how we teach and learn and live. As a classroom teacher I believe it is important that we approach our teaching practice in this manner—remembering we are always learners at the same time that we are teachers. The more we are able to view our work as teachers this way, the more we will begin to discover the poetry of our lives, both in and outside the classroom.

Clearing the Land

September in Arizona is a long way from autumn. In other parts of
the country leaves begin to turn red and chilly winds signal the
changing seasons. Sweaters are unpacked, and a crispness permeates
the air. Where we live in the desert, though, it's still just plain hot.
That's how it was the day we began our garden adventure.

One afternoon I read Roxaboxen, Alice McLerran's book
about a group of children who create their own desert community.
Then everyone raced out of the classroom, ready to spend the
afternoon preparing the space we planned to inhabit each Wednes-
day afternoon for the rest of the school year. This bit of land,
adjacent to our building, had been the school garden for the past
several years. We inherited it because nobody wanted to plant
another garden.

The area was overrun with weeds and needed attention.
Leftovers from the previous year's garden remained, thick-rooted
plants that had all gone to seed. Our first task was to remove the
grass that had almost completely taken over; it was nearly as tall as
some of the children. A few of the children jumped right into pulling
grass and enthusiastically piled it into plastic bags to haul to the
dumpster. We startled a colony of ants residing in the rich soil, and
they responded with bites on small hands and feet. While the grass
pullers were busy at their jobs (including trips to the office for
calamine lotion), other children opted for a cooler solution to the day
by chatting casually under a shade tree. Still others discovered palo
verde seeds and began collecting them for "money." Later that day

we went back inside, red-faced with sweat dripping down, thoroughly hot, yet inspired.

In the days that followed, parents arrived with cement blocks and boards they had cleaned out of their garages. One day Mikey's mom walked into the room with his little brother's baby stroller full of red bricks. Bryan returned from a weekend at the beach in Mexico with a box of shells to share. News of our project spread around the school, and all sorts of castaway items showed up miraculously as treasures for us to use. Poetry was the furthest thing from any of our minds when we began this outdoor adventure; but like a poem, once the inspiration has arrived, there is no holding back its expression.

T he inspiration for the garden project (as I came to call it, although there was no traditional gardening involved) had its roots in my childhood. Summer days of flooding a backyard ditch with neighborhood children gave us experiences with nature that I will never forget. As we constructed our own little community of mud, sand, and water, we tried to make sense of the world by creating our own. Another summer childhood experience—sailing in northern Minnesota—furthered my efforts to make sense of my life. Learning to sail taught me to find that delicate and exhilarating point of balance between wind and water—"the edge," as I called it—where I was able to travel if I was willing to take the risk and stay wide awake to its possibilities. It was during those days, immersed in natural elements, that I was first inspired as a poet. Poetry became my means of self-expression and self-discovery.

Remembering those two experiences with the natural world and the influence they had on my life, I could see possibilities held by the hot, weedy plot of earth outside our school. Although I wasn't thinking of poets at the time, perhaps in the back of my mind I realized that if I provided my students the opportunity to work and play close to the land, maybe it would somehow move them along "the edge" as learners and inspire them as poets. If nothing else, I thought it would give them a chance to interact with the earth and each other in new, enriching ways similar to those I experienced growing up. It seemed quite possible that if we cleared the land, it could make a space for something wonderful to happen.

The Greek word for truth, *aletheia,* literally means a "clearing." H. H. the Dalai Lama says, "Truth is sensed as something that emerges as we enter a clearing where the obscuring clouds of ignorance, prejudice, and fear have, at least momentarily, been lifted." He adds further: "This is something that can only be done step by step, moment by moment. It means staying in touch with the delicate balance that friendship requires, above all the balance between speaking and listening" (1990, 13). Although I anticipated the possibilities for interpersonal growth in our outdoor "clearing," it wasn't until later that the connection with poetry was made. Louise Chawla (1994) explores the relationship between nature, poetry, and childhood memory in her book *In the First Country of Places.* She draws from the work of Martin Heidegger, a German philosopher who also reflected upon the notion of truth and its relationship to the idea of clearing. "Truth, Heidegger argued . . . is an occurrence, when a person and something perceived come together in a 'clearing' in which the thing (another person, an object, a place) is given freedom to reveal itself . . . He maintained that we create a clearing and approach the truth of things most closely through the receptive language of poetry" (17). Heidegger's own words offer additional clarification: "Only this clearing grants and guarantees to us humans a passage to those beings that we ourselves are not, and access to the being that we ourselves are" (1971, 53). Furthermore, Chawla views her own work as an effort "to create a clearing—an open space in which all attention is focused on hearing and understanding" (1994, 50).

As a teacher of young poets, I find this notion of creating a clearing for truth and understanding to occur particularly significant. It requires us to make a shift in our own thinking and practices, to make a space for the kind of learning that occurs when children become poets. When I think of the idea of clearing, one of the first thoughts that comes to mind is the removal of debris or any unnecessary matter that might inhibit growth. It is the time when dirt clods are broken down so they can support what will sprout rather than get in the way. In the classroom where young poets grow, this is analogous to opening ourselves to the possibilities of working with children and poetry, and letting go of our own fears and hesitations about the process. It is the point in our work where we must seek the support of those who can guide us, and begin taking risks ourselves, both as teachers and writers. Establishing a clearing at which poetry may arrive requires us to consider the following:

◆   *Not all poets are alike.* Some people are natural poets, endowed at birth with everything necessary to give the world the verses it demands. Like a seed that carries the germ of life within it, a natural poet needs only the proper conditions and care for writing poems. A true poet's gift arrives with his or her first breath. True poets are the beautiful wildflowers that will bloom nearly anywhere without much effort. Trying is rarely involved, the poetry is already there. Other poets have to learn their craft. They are the ones who have to work harder to write the poetry of their lives, and the tools of the trade—notebooks, computers, anthologies of other writers, techniques, and various other inspirations, especially teachers—play a more important role. These poets need someone to remove the overgrown grass and help sow their seeds. They need careful tending and a watchful gardener to make sure conditions for growth are just right. Regardless of how we arrive at poetry, we can adjust and include practices in our daily lives—both in and outside of the classroom—which will enable poetry and poets to flourish.

◆   *We must welcome the poet within ourselves and make a place for poetry in our lives.* Like the gardener who first clears a space for plants, this happens by initially accepting the fact that living the poet's life is often a lonely

venture. Many potential poets resist writing poetry because it requires a significant amount of time alone for
reflection, observation, and contemplation. It demands we
find just the right word for that which is often impossible
to say. Poetry writing takes us deep inside ourselves to
places we sometimes never expect to go, places that are
scary or uncertain where no one else can accompany us.
It insists that we leave part of our worldly self behind as
we enter the territory where poetry resides. We have to be
willing to enter those solitary spaces in order to find the
poet who will usher us to the words waiting to be written.
And once our writing is completed, we are faced with
deciding if and how we want to make it available to
others. Kathleen Norris (1996) writes, "Art is a lonely
calling, and yet paradoxically communal. If artists invent
themselves, it is in the service of others. The work of my
life is given to others; in fact the reader completes it" (43).

◆　*As poets we have to realize that at times we may be
opening ourselves up to intense struggles and vulnerabili-
ties.* A poet lives with passion and an acute view of the
world. The joys felt are intensely joyful, and the experience of human suffering is nearly unbearable at times. A
poet must be willing to know the highest of highs and the
lowest of lows, and try to make sense of what appears at
times to make no sense at all.

◆　*Being a poet demands wide-awakeness.* When we come
to a clearing made available for poetry, we must be ready
to respond appropriately. Like the children who discovered geckos and worms during our first few weeks outside
in the garden, we must be constantly alert for the poetry
tucked away in surprising places of our lives. Lines for a
poem come from watching an elderly woman nibbling
gumdrops from a plastic bag as she reads on the airplane,
en route to see her daughter. Or from the scent of a baby
lingering on her grandmother's shirt as she drives away
across the desert. A poet's work is to pay attention to these
moments, write them down, and acknowledge them as
poetry. Later, when the time is right, they will be trans-

formed into poems, helping others to see what ordinarily goes unseen.

◆ *The life of a poet requires patience.* It demands an alertness to possibilities and, at the same time, a willingness to wait until a poem takes full shape, until it is ready. A poem may lie dormant for months and then nag relentlessly at the poet until it is written down. Poetry pulls us away from the world until we write what must be written, often shoving everything else aside until each word, space, or line is exactly right; it doesn't always happen at the most convenient time. Although poetry demands much of those who choose to write, it also generously gives something back in return. The unsettled feeling before a poem is just right is often replaced by a sense of balance once the poem is completed. The initial feeling of being pulled away into loneliness is transformed into a sense of oneness with life without separation. It's just enough to keep a poet inspired and writing.

◆ *The life of a poet is not an occasional task—it is a way of being.* It requires an inner discipline, an awakened eye, an eager hand ready to record poetic moments. Preparing ourselves for our work as poets calls us to make a shift in the way we live our lives. Regardless if we choose poetry as our main profession, as something we do when we can, or if we want to use it in our classrooms with children, it is important to acknowledge what poetry demands and what it is capable of giving us. If we are willing to make it a part of our lives, we are opening up vast opportunities for more clear understanding of ourselves as human beings. When we take the time to observe what *is* more acutely, it will help us also to visualize what could be and should be.

Taking on the responsibility of including poetry in our students' lives carries significant implications. It requires that we sharpen our observational skills as we teach our young students to do the same. It asks us to see the potential in their writing and guide them gently along their way as poets. Welcoming the poet in each of our students requires us to know when to offer suggestions and when to say nothing. It forces us to give them time to find their poetry and figure out a way to commit it to printed form. It involves a deep trust between student and teacher. We have to remember that the seed gatherers and the children chatting peacefully under the shade tree are clearing a space for their work as much as those who are hauling off bags of weeds to the trash. Helping our students become poets, if we do it well, calls us to step aside and open ourselves to the important messages carried in their poems and how they write them. For in encouraging them to express what they observe and know, we are potentially exposing ourselves to our own shortcomings and at the same time asking them for guidance and a vision for our future.

When the idea came to use the garden space for an outdoor experience, I had a few thoughts about how it might unfold. I thought, perhaps, I could structure it so that we'd have a year of science topics to study, using the outdoor time as a starting point for lessons in ecology, life science, geology, etc. After one or two sessions, I realized that the most important thing I could do was "clear out" of their way, pay attention, and stay open to what they had to teach me. The approach I took was similar to the way I have worked with them as poets.

Clearing a space for our students' poetry requires that we first clear a space for our own. Even if we never choose to share our poetry with others, we still need to step through the door and make ourselves familiar with the poet who will be charged with the task of bringing other poets, especially young ones, along. It requires us to get our hands dirty and remove the overgrown weeds and dirt clods of our lives, knowing we may receive a few ant bites in the process. We must each reflect on our own journey as a poet if we want to be the best guide we can be for those who will depend on us for assistance. In doing this, we will be wiser and more attuned to what lies before us as teachers, opening up a wealth of possibilities for seeing our lives from a new perspective—through the eyes of young poets—and perhaps respond in a way that can make a difference.

CHAPTER TWO

A Watchful Gardener

Growing plants has never been one of my strengths. If I want them to survive, I hand them over to someone else who knows how to keep them alive. It's a matter of recognizing who has a talent for something and then taking advantage of their gift. I learned this lesson repeatedly in our garden that grew just about everything but plants.

At eight, Kinley is one of those students who gets an idea and won't let it go until the people around him, particularly his teachers, have done everything possible to see that his idea reaches fruition. Inspired by an abundance of mud and absence of plants in the rich soil, he somehow got it into his head that he wanted to build an adobe house. While most of his peers were satisfied to make mud balls and soupy mixtures, he had bigger ideas. He wanted to construct a house in which he could actually sit. After considerable negotiations, we talked him into making a model adobe. In order to construct it properly, we called in an expert for a training session. We invited Bill (my husband, a former construction manager) to give us a few tips on how to build with mud.

Bill joined us one Friday morning to talk to the class about adobe. He asked if anyone knew what mortar was, and Kinley said, "It's the stuff that sticks stones together." Bill talked about plaster that you put on the outside of adobe blocks and said it's kind of like pudding. Denise chuckled and said, "We wouldn't eat it!" Caitlin added, "I don't think plaster would be your average milk pudding!"

Bill described how the Hopis have a ceremony in which the women put back on the walls the mud that has slipped down from

8

the rain falling on it. He told us about a building in Iran that a
family has lived in continuously for four thousand years. As he
explained the process of building with adobe, Denise commented,
"So what you're saying is you put a lot of rocks together and glue
them together."

He told us that we'd need to work with caliche, pure dirt,
which has no organic matter in it. Bill explained how to keep the
blocks straight when building and how they have to be offset. He told
us that putting the plaster on the outside is like frosting a birthday
cake and suggested that anyone interested in making a model house
should draw up a plan. He returned a few weeks later, after all
interested builders had drawn their plans.

He showed us how to sweep clean the concrete space where
we'd do our mixing and presented the necessary tools for making
adobe blocks: the form for the blocks, a trowel, and the "masher."
Bill also brought three buckets of dirt and told us it was "just like
making pancakes." As he demonstrated, he explained how you have
to get rid of the clods before putting in the rest of the water, and how
when it dries it will be like cement. While Bill stirred the slippery
mixture, there were numerous comments about his work, including
one of the kids calling it a "messterpiece."

Bill poured some of the excess water out of the bucket into a
small cup. Everyone was immediately interested in it, and this
conversation followed:

Teagan: Others say "yuck" [about the cup of muddy water], Tasha
and I say, "Cool!" Say you lived in Buffalo in winter,
would your adobe freeze?
Bill: You wouldn't have adobe in Buffalo because the soil is too
loamy.
Teagan: What if you brought it from somewhere else?
Bill: I couldn't tell you.
Erik: How long does it take to dry?
Bill: We don't know. It's an experiment. I messed with it when I
was in construction—that's what construction guys call it when
you work with this stuff—messed.
Oliver: Were you a construction guy once?

Realizing we had just about reached our limit for sitting still and *watching, Bill finished up the demonstration and then suggested that Kinley do some himself. Kinley wanted to work alone, although several others wanted to help. Bryan ended up hanging around to help him, and in the months that followed, they made hundreds of one-inch adobe blocks for their own model houses. Additionally, they set up a training course for others who wanted to learn. This rigorous course required that each trainee assist with three batches and then make one independently before "graduating" from adobe school.*

Like most teachers of young children, I never attended poetry school, never studied with the great poets of our times or even read the classics required of all serious poetry students. I didn't participate in a training course where, like with the adobe, I was required to mix up a batch of poems under the scrutiny of a wise teacher before being sent off to make my own. My "messing" with poetry grew out of experiences with the natural world, the children I spend each school day with, and other writers I know who struggle as I do to find a way to say what is in their hearts and minds. I have learned to be a poet through writing poetry, through staying with a poem long enough to select the words or phrases that convey my exact intended meaning. I have learned to be a poet through reading the lines of other poets, young and old, who have learned to see the world through poetry and have written it all down. I have become a poet through befriending solitude—so that in silence my inner voice can be heard.

Poetry has come naturally for me. I may not possess all of the technical skills to be a great poet, but since early in my life I've always viewed the world through a poet's eyes. The solitary time I spent as a child awakened a profound longing to understand life's deeper truths. I saw things differently than most children with whom I grew up and often felt isolated and alone. Kathleen Norris writes: "When artists discover as children that they have inappropriate responses to events around them, they also find, as they learn to trust those responses, that these oddities are what constitute their value to others" (1996, 39). It took me well into my adulthood to understand this. As a child I was actively connected to the earth and the natural world. Grasses of the Nebraska plains, clay excavated from nearby hillsides, and the wind rippling across northern Minnesota lakes were among my most treasured companions and earliest mentors. Being outside so much, especially when I was alone, helped me see that we are all connected to something larger than our individual selves. My experiences with the natural world inspired many questions:

◆ What is our purpose for being?
◆ Where do I fit into the greater scheme of things?
◆ What is most important in life?

Parallel to my outdoor play and contemplation of life's truths, I was an avid reader. As I entered adolescence, I was intrigued by writers who allowed me to see their inner worlds filled with the same struggles I was experiencing. Writers like Antoine de Saint-Exupéry and Langston Hughes drew me in and invited me to begin writing my own poetry. Their words found a strong place in my heart, and even when I felt lonely and separate from the people around me, it was a comfort to know that there were others who had similar thoughts and dreams. They inspired me to continue my quest for understanding as I began my own journey as a poet.

In my young adulthood, I was influenced as a poet by the lyrics of Bob Dylan, Joni Mitchell, Judy Collins, Joan Baez, and Leonard Cohen. Their powerful words, written and sung to convey their messages in response to turbulent times, remain with me as an inspiration to keep saying what needs to be said. They sparked a passion for asking the hard questions and then going about finding answers. Their words gave me courage to push myself and not look back. As I became more serious about writing poetry, their verses encouraged a sense of bravery in my own.

I've kept a journal since around age twelve, but a writer's notebook became a more serious venture in my early twenties. As I read more poetry and began to fill pages with my own lines, I also was led to a teacher, Erma Pounds, who taught me not about poetry, but about a way to practice being quiet within myself. Over twenty years of meditation practice have helped me feel more at home with solitude. I have learned to enter the inner poet's territory with more grace and understanding. My poet's voice is clearer and stronger because I've learned to listen to it and commit its message to the page.

My work as a teacher came shortly after I began seriously keeping a writing journal, and poetry naturally followed. As I practiced listening to my inner voice, I also began listening to the voices of children. For years I heard their stories and helped them by simply taking dictation. What they said, I recorded. Then in the mid-1980s, about the time Donald Graves's (1983) work on writing process was becoming known around the country, a group of local teachers and university professors organized courses to promote holistic educational practices and to support teachers in implementing such practices in their classrooms. These courses provided a whole new lens through which to view children's writing and literacy development. I began to see how literature, poetry, writing, and other means of expression all contribute to a child's literate self. I realized that for children to be writers, they need to be immersed in the sounds of the best literature, and it was my job as their teacher to provide that and help them make the connection between the two. In addition to filling their daily lives with wonderful books, stories, and poetry, I also began to understand how I could proactively help them develop their craft as writers.

For several years much of our writing focus in the classroom was on personal narrative. Mary Ellen Giacobbe, the teacher in whose classroom Donald Graves did his research, helped lay a strong foundation for writing practice through her classroom demonstrations. She modeled so well how to listen to children and respond in a receptive, encouraging manner. Having the opportunity to learn directly from Mary Ellen raised the writing and literacy development in my classroom to a new level. It was supported further over the next few years by the work of Graves, Shelley Harwayne, Lucy Calkins, Nancie Atwell, Ken and Yetta Goodman, Frank Smith, and eventually Georgia Heard and Ralph Fletcher. We were fortunate to have had many of these teachers make presentations in our area. Their wisdom enhanced that of our local mentors and helped holistic practices to flourish in many nearby schools.

My work as a teacher of writing progressed successfully. I was able to draw creative stories out of my young students, and we were excited about the wonderful work we did together each day in school. As with all good writing, our work as writers was always full of surprises. There was one surprise, however, for which I was completely unprepared. It has taken me years to recognize its full impact on my writing life.

In February of 1989, Donald Murray and his wife Minnie Mae came to Arizona for a month. They came so Don could teach a series of writing workshops to local teachers and writers, and so Minnie Mae, as it turned out, could pick fresh grapefruit from a tree in her backyard each morning. My experience with Don is best described by this "one-pager" I was asked later to write about him:

> I never expected to be a writer so profoundly influenced by a man who buys shirts at a truck stop. Was it news that Arizona truck stops were well supplied that drew him to the desert? Was it the prospect of facing another New England February? Or was it something else—a knowing, perhaps, that writers out West were searching for lines, just as he was searching for shirts?
>
> It was February, 1989, when Don and Minnie Mae journeyed our way. That same month my first published article appeared in *Language Arts*. Needless to say, I felt more than a little pleased with myself for having reached such a milestone in my career. I believed I had arrived as a writer, and thought a few sessions with Donald Murray would further my writing skills. Anticipating nothing more than writing tips, I was unprepared for the impact he would have on my life.

For four weeks we arrived at his Saturday workshop, pens and notebooks in hand. We wrote and shared our work. We talked about writing. Don gave us tips:

- Get your rear end in the chair every day.
- Write a draft, even if it's bad writing—you can revise it later.
- Find the line.
- Be true to your own voice.
- Stick your writing in the mail.

I wrote down his tips with passion and swallowed my pride when he suggested a change to a poem I wrote, a poem I thought was perfect. Vowing to do everything I could to craft my writing like Don's, I aspired to be a great writer.

Then one morning as he struggled with his own writing, Don told us a story about the western shirts he likes to wear which are available only at truck stops. He told us when he finds them he usually buys several so he'll have a good supply. At that moment, everything shifted for me. I realized that this extraordinary writer was just an ordinary man. A man who frequents truck stops to buy shirts and a writer who, like myself, wrestles with grumpy moods, a fidgety body, and days of bad writing.

Don's story became the line for all of my future work. It reminded me that we don't have to try to be great writers or produce literary masterpieces. What we need to do is pay attention to the details of ordinary life and write about them in ways that are true to our own voices. When we make this a lifetime practice, we begin to see what is right before us and accept it for what it is. If we stay with it long enough, we might even surprise ourselves and write something extraordinary. Like shirts at a truck stop, the lines of our lives are waiting to be found if we slow down long enough to notice them.

Donald Murray changed my life. Although I had been a writer before I met him, he showed me how to live the writer's life. Through his example, I was able to find my voice and realize that to be writers we have to allow our passions and obsessions to be our allies. He quickly became the wise and watchful gardener I needed to help me tend my blossoming garden of words.

Don made me a meticulous critic of my writing, not allowing any unnecessary or imprecise words to be included.

He also encouraged me to write badly at first, just to get a draft written to move the process along. Donald Murray taught me the importance of carrying a daybook at all times, and using it to record the details of everyday living that catch us by surprise and often go unnoticed. He taught me to stay with writing, for better or for worse, and to be patient with myself when I felt like being impatient. As my teacher, Don gave me permission to revisit important topics and to continue to learn from them. He inspired me to always try to make my best better, and to have the confidence in my writing to share it with others.

Although my time with Donald Murray was brief, he remains with me each and every moment that I write. His teachings affect my writing and the writing of my students. As I've learned to fill the pages of my writer's notebook with life's quirky details, I have encouraged the children I work with to do the same. As my writer's view of the world has grown, so have theirs.

Of all his teachings about writing, the most significant one for me has been the notion of "finding the line." Murray writes, "The line is a word or a series of words that points toward a potential meaning. . . . The line is often made up of code words that have private meanings that appear general, vague, or cliché to other readers but which are loaded with precise meanings for the writer" (Murray 1989, 41). As I've thought about this idea of "finding the line," I've realized what he was telling us is that, regardless of what we are writing, we always need to be in search of the words, phrases, or ideas which cut to the quick of what we're trying to say. We should always be on the alert for words which speak directly and precisely to the truth of the matter at hand, the words that draw us into the "clearings" (see Chapter 1) of our lives. Finding the line also has implications for teaching beyond writing. When I am planning a course of study at the beginning of the year, for example, deciding what the "line" will be is important. Establishing the ideas and concepts most true to what I want my students to learn sets a firm foundation for all learning that follows. When the line is right, it is always accompanied by a clear sense of knowing.

Murray's influence on my writing life has been far-reaching. His teachings, through words and example, permanently altered the way I have conducted my life as a teacher and writer. He gave me the confidence to push harder, work more courageously, and take risks as a writer that I wouldn't have taken before. His influence helped move my writing into a more public arena and encouraged me to keep sharing what I have learned through my published work. Donald Murray reminds me that what I have to say is worthwhile and that I have a responsibility to pass on to others what I have learned from the wise teachers with whom I've been fortunate to study.

The month I spent learning from Don Murray created a significant shift in my life. After I met Don I committed myself to being a writer. Although I knew my time for writing would have to be shared with other responsibilities such as teaching, my family, and artistic interests, I felt a growing passion for writing that has remained since Don's visit to the desert. In time that passion for writing, especially writing poetry, was fed by another teacher who also found her way to the desert, and to my heart.

I first met Georgia Heard in the spring of 1991. She came to Arizona to give a poetry workshop for teachers and children. As I listened to Georgia speak about poetry in her gentle, thoughtful voice, I knew I'd found a kindred spirit. I also knew I had met a teacher who would guide me as a poet and teacher of poetry.

Over the next several years, Georgia made annual trips to Arizona, and I attended her classroom demonstrations on numerous occasions. Each time I watched her delicately draw lines of poetry from both eager and reluctant young poets, I gained new insight into how to do the same in my own classroom. I was impressed by her ideas about poetry, such as giving poetry to students like flowers so they could look at the world in a different way. The expressions on the children's

faces as they sat beside her and shared their poems was
poetry itself.

Once in a while, Georgia gave workshops just for
grown-ups. During these sessions she reminded us of the role
trust plays in the development of a poet. Georgia had a way of
helping us each open the door to the places inside ourselves
where poems reside. Her unhurried, reflective pace gave us
time to search for the right words we wanted to use to say
what was in our hearts. She gave us examples of other poets'
work to show specifically how they used imagery, rhythm,
and metaphor, and to hear the sounds of their voices. Georgia
gave us a quiet, safe space in which to take risks as poets, and
to share our voices as she shared her own.

Knowing Georgia—both through her workshops and as a
personal friend—inspired me to stay with my writing when I
became discouraged. She, like Don Murray, lives the life of a
writer, and offered another version of what that life can look
like. Georgia works from the heart and has continually
reminded me to do the same. Her gentleness inspires those
she teaches to look deeper within themselves for the poetry
that is there. Her work has helped me see how poetry can be
a powerful tool for self-discovery. She has taught me to
remain a vigilant observer of what is in my heart and to
always be ready to write it down. Georgia set an example for
how to live in a way that poems will be found and has shown
me that if I can ascertain the truth of my life through poetry, it
will lead to truth in other ways as well.

Although I have spent less time with him directly, I have
also been mentored in important ways by Ralph Fletcher.
Through his books on writing and a handful of conversations
over the past several years, Ralph has encouraged me to work
at the craft of writing and to develop the writer's notebook as
a powerful tool. He has reminded me also of the importance
of mentors who are willing to set high standards for their
students and then allow them to discover their own voices. In
What a Writer Needs (1993) he writes: "A mentor possesses
an inner honesty, an ability to recognize that the novice's

different style of writing may camouflage a deeper truth: The novice writes better than the teacher. It requires courage and real humility to recognize this and step graciously out of the way" (16). Ralph has helped me be patient and compassionate with myself as a writer, and with my students.

I have been fortunate to have these fine mentors (and many others not mentioned in this current work) who have guided and inspired me to keep filling the pages of my writer's notebook. They, and the solitude I've known through the natural world, have all been influential teachers. I have had other teachers as well, who continue to show me every day where there is poetry in my life. These teachers are the children with whom I write and read and learn in my classroom. They push me to know more, to see more, to write what I observe in new ways. Their lives and their ideas are poetry in motion, and they've shown me what is important and worthy of my attention. Ralph Fletcher describes this relationship well: "Through the relationship with a novice, the mentor gets to experience the thrill of the craft (as well as its pain) all over again. In this way the mentor's passion never gets spent: it gets renewed again and again through the mentoring relationship" (1993, 18).

Daily life with my students has nurtured me both as a writer and as a teacher. Our daily living and learning together have taught me the value of practice and the power of its accumulated effect. As both teacher and student simultaneously, we have become adobe makers and poets together.

CHAPTER THREE

A Safe Place to Grow

Before long there were all kinds of growth in our garden. But instead of neat rows of carrots and radishes, we had other things growing. The children used anything they could get their hands on to make their houses. Bricks, river rocks, chicken wire, and walls of mud were soon transformed into personal residences. Baby food jars filled with colored water scattered a rainbow around our garden as varied and beautiful as the children who created it. An entrepreneurial spirit took over.

The palo verde tree overlooking our space produced thousands of seeds, which immediately became our currency. Children bought and sold everything from bricks and ceramic tiles to handmade comic books. Some children even worked for "money" by offering to dig mud, haul sand, or help a friend set up his or her house. Capitalism flourished. We made up community policy as we went along, and when someone approached the limits of what we thought was acceptable, we met as a group to decide the proper course of action. One day we reached that point when children began bringing toys from home to sell.

Mary: What do you think about people bringing toys to sell?
Teagan: The whole garden is a toy.
Indra: It's a nature place, a nature toy. Some toys are wood. It's nature. Plastic isn't nature.
Andréa: Toys aren't really helpful. Toys sit there and get dusty and get cobwebs.
Erik: The big difference is that toys are to play with and tools are to work with.

After a brief discussion of other issues, the discussion moved back to the toys:

Erik: It's okay to sell but toys would melt.

Caitlin: It could rot.
Jesse: The person who bought it would be mad (because they didn't
　　　get a good one).
Kinley: Plastic doesn't go back to the earth.

Eventually we arrived at a unanimous decision: No toys in the
garden. This conversation was the foundation for a policy that
remained solid throughout the year. A month or so later, two boys
requested an opportunity to make and sell toys. Because the toys
were handmade, I thought the class might bend a bit on the "no
toys" rule. I was surprised by their response. Someone mentioned
that the wind would be a problem and if the toys blew away they'd
have to get their money back. Someone else said the rain might be a
problem. Tasha said, "We're not going to be playing out there, we
have a lot of work to do." Indra added, "The garden is not a place
for plastic stuff that couldn't go into the earth. It doesn't decom-
pose."
　　Kinley proposed letting them try it out. He said, "It would be
fair to take them out if they bring them back to the room." Then we
discussed the problem of storage and whether or not they could keep
them in their cubbyholes, mailboxes, or drying rack area. I was
leaning toward going with Kinley's suggestion, but I didn't say
anything. I suggested we have a vote about whether or not to have
the toys out there. One of the children reminded me that we already
have a rule about that, so we voted instead whether or not to follow
the rule. It was an overwhelming 17 to 2 vote—the two toymakers
being the only ones voting not to follow the rule. I was impressed by
the children's commitment to what had already been established and
their dedication to maintaining the garden order.

Discussions such as these helped set up the ethical
standards within our democratic classroom society.
The order enabled everyone to know what to expect
and how to respond accordingly. It helped all community
members find their place within the group and to feel safe.
The predictable nature of a community established in this
manner helped make it successful.

　　This kind of community building and maintenance was
important for our outdoor work. It is also important when

working with a group of young poets. I have learned from experience that for writers to succeed, they need to know that they are writing in safe territory. If they are worried about their work being criticized publicly or privately, they won't produce much more than superficial nonsense. When they feel a lack of support from their teachers and peers, they will seldom risk revealing the poet within themselves.

For young poets to thrive, they need the proper conditions. Like tender young plants poking their earliest shoots up from the soil, they will thrive if handled with gentle care and attention. Similar to the gardener who keeps a constant vigil to maintain an optimum growing environment, the teacher plays a central role in this aspect of the process. It requires adoption of a new paradigm, a shift in thinking, before teaching practices can be considered. To successfully help young children become poets, these ideas need to be contemplated:

◆ *The teacher must be a writer, too.* I have been most successful as a poetry teacher when I've let my students know from the beginning that I am a writer also. When they write, I write alongside them. They see me filling the pages of my writer's notebook as they are beginning to fill theirs. I become their equal in this way, and although I maintain my role as their teacher and guide, I am just one writer among many. As with the discussion about toys in the garden, I have my opinion but model for them that I am just as interested in hearing what they have to say as I am in expressing my own thoughts. They see me writing, and it encourages them to want to be writers, too.

◆ *Revealing our process as writers is essential.* I have found it helpful to show my students examples of drafts of my poems and final versions. I talk to my students about how I get ideas for poems and what I'm struggling with in a poem. I read them lines I have written and tell stories about how I arrived at a certain poem. I make myself available to them in a deeper sense, and demonstrate ways in which I am just as vulnerable as they are. For

example, two summers ago I received news that my
daughter and her husband were expecting a baby. I was in
Montana at the time visiting friends, and that whole night
after I found out about the baby I kept thinking about my
daughter when she was first born. She had a soft, dark
fuzz all over her back, forehead, ears, and shoulders. She
reminded me of a little bear. The next morning when I
woke up, there was a black bear in our friends' yard. As
we drove away from our friends' cabin, I scribbled down
words to remember how I felt in that moment (Figure 1).
After I returned home the draft became this poem:

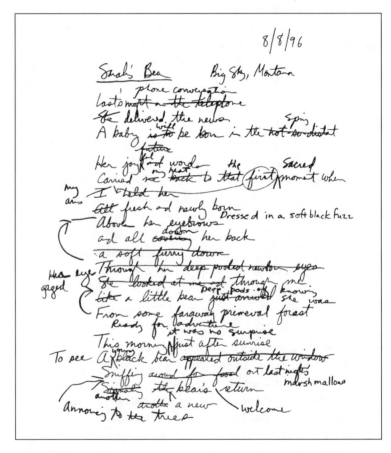

Figure 1

Sarah's Bear
Big Sky, Montana

Last night's phone conversation
Delivered her news
A baby will arrive in the spring
Her joyful words carried my heart
To the first sacred moment
When my arms held her
Fresh and newly born

Dressed in a soft black fuzz
Above her eyebrows
And all down her back
Her eyes gazed through me like
Deep pools of knowing
From some faraway primeval forest
A little bear she was
Ready for adventure

This morning it was no surprise then
Just after sunrise
To see a young black bear
Sniffing out last night's marshmallows
Announcing to the trees
Another bear's welcome return

It seemed important that my students see my rough draft
as well as the final product. I wanted them to see my
original thinking and images, and notice how they shifted
once I had a chance to revise the poem. I wanted my
students to have a glimpse into my process and see one of
the most important subjects in my life: my love for my
daughters, and their growing up and moving on into their
own lives. Certainly some of my poetry isn't appropriate
to share with second graders, but much of it is, and they
can benefit from a glimpse into another writer's thinking
and composing process.

◆ *To be good writing teachers we have to be willing to meet
our students on equal ground.* When I write with my
students and share my struggles and joys as a writer with
them, it sets us on equal ground. My age and experience

give me a different perspective, of course, but by opening up my process to my students, as I did with the poem about the bear, I am removing myself from a position of control, of always being the one providing the information and directions. When I sit at a table quietly writing beside my students, and later listen to them talk about their own writing as I did mine, I am sending the message that I am here to learn from them and listen to their responses just as much as I want them to hear what I have to say. When I am trying to help them with their writing, the examples of my own work become a reference point for learning about their own writing process. This kind of arrangement helps children to feel more trusting and willing to write from their hearts. When they see other writers seriously working at their practice, even the most reluctant writers will usually give it a try. One poet inspires another, and before long a whole classroom of poets is growing.

◆ *A predictable routine is integral to a strong poetry writing program.* Establishing and maintaining a safe environment for young writers can only happen by providing a predict-able routine. Good poetry won't happen if it's only presented as an assignment once a month or even once a week. Young poets need to know that at a consistent time nearly every day they will be given the opportunity to write, to share their work, to illustrate, and celebrate their writing accomplishments. As young as they are, they will begin to plan their writing projects on their own if they know the time will be there for them to do all the things writers need to do. Chapter 4 examines in detail the application of daily writing practice with young poets.

◆ *Time to think is as important as time to write.* Another way in which time comes into play is allowing children the space to think about what they want to say without expecting them to fill their pages quickly and fully every time they sit down. Particularly for children who are reluctant to commit themselves to print, this kind of time is invaluable. I remember one student, Bryan, who sat for nearly two weeks with his blank writing notebook in front of him. I sat beside Bryan and gently asked him questions about his pets, family interests, vacations, and anything I could think of to get him to put something on his paper. I suggested different ideas based on what I knew about him, thinking that would get him started. Nothing. Finally, I decided to back off and leave him alone for a few days. I told Bryan, "I can tell you need more time to think about your writing. I'm trusting you'll put some words in your writer's notebook when you're ready." I felt it was important not to even mention the word *poem* with Bryan at that point, because it seemed like the idea of writing a poem was adding even more pressure to his anxiety about writing. The next two or three days were a test for me to stay out of Bryan's way. Just when I was about ready to give up, he surprised me with this poem:

Cobra

Cobra is my
dog when I give
him a bath after that he
zooooms down
stairs I try to catch
him but he's too
fast after his
bath.

Not only had Bryan written, but he had written well. He captured the excitement of giving his dog a bath and the futility of trying to catch him afterward. When I read his poem I not only felt happy for him and proud, but was reminded of the importance of allowing the kind of time I gave Bryan to find his writer's voice. In many respects, I didn't feel I could take any credit for his wonderful poem. Yet I doubt that he would have written at all unless he knew I trusted him and was willing to allow him time to feel safe and secure enough within to write a poem.

◆ *Trust is a must for poetry to grow.* The trust and security that grow when time is given for young poets' voices to be discovered are the foundation of a good writing program for children. Trust occurs when children know their teacher will support them in their sincere writing efforts. Although Bryan was hesitant to write a poem initially, he knew through my words and actions that I trusted him as a writer. In turn, he came to trust himself as a poet and take the risk of revealing his thoughts on paper. This happened in part because he also trusted that I would honor and celebrate his work, rather than criticize it. Trust is an element that pervades a classroom where poetry is alive—without it I doubt that any writing could be much more than superficial. In many respects it is like the water needed to sustain a garden. The proper timing and amount are crucial to the garden's continued growth.

When the conditions for a garden are as perfect as can be—rich, tilled soil, natural sunlight, a reliable source of available water, seeds conducive to growth in the designated climate—the rest is up to the gardener. So it is with teachers of young poets. Once time and trust are established, through daily practices and our own efforts to model what writers do, the voices will become clear and strong. Poets will emerge long before they even know they are poets. This happened one day in October after I'd read a section from Georgia Heard's *Writing toward Home* (1995) called "Listening to the Corn." She described a day when she sat listening to the wind moving through a dried-up cornfield at the end of summer. She suggested trying to listen to the sounds of the world around us in a new way. Shortly after we read Georgia's piece and talked briefly about it, we went out to our garden area. It was windy and there was a subtle hint of fall in the air. We all sat down with our writing notebooks and listened to the wind, the traffic in the street, and to the leaves rustling about. Some of the children took a while to get settled, but eventually everyone wrote without difficulty. I wrote too, and after I'd finished a poem I looked around at the beautiful children in my class, all seriously taking on their life as a poet. Chelsea, a delicate, soft-spoken child, wrote this poem as she sat in her shady spot against the fence (Figure 2):

I am sitting on a rock
Peacefully writing my
thoughts with the wind
blowing in my face in the
fall with two days in the
middle of today and
my birthday thinking what
fun I'll have on that day.
I love just sitting on a
rock not talking to anybody
writing my thoughts on a
nice fall day in a spot
that's mine.

In her poem, Chelsea captured the feeling of the day, the
gentleness of the wind, the joy of having her own quiet space

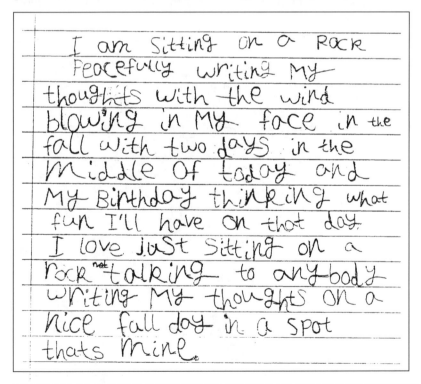

Figure 2

for writing and thinking, and the anticipation of her approaching birthday. In that quiet moment of reflection and writing, she also found her voice.

As teachers who tend crops of young poets, it is our responsibility to give our students opportunities such as this one to find their voices within a community of writers. Additionally, as the poems are written, students need to know that it is safe to share their work with an audience who will be receptive. Committing thoughts and feelings to the page is one thing, sharing writing publicly is another. A significant part of establishing a nurturing poetry environment is modeling how to give helpful and supportive responses to what has been written. I always try to start with what I see as the poem's strength and what the writer has done to say something in a unique way. I will use Keith's poem (Figure 3) about his friend Taylor as an example:

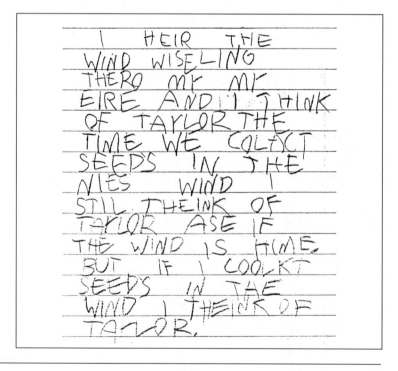

Figure 3

I hear the
wind whistling
through my
ear and I think
of Taylor the
time we collect(ed)
seeds in the
nice wind I
still think of
Taylor as if
the wind is him.
But if I collect
seeds in the
wind I think of
Taylor.

I always try to begin with a line that jumps out at me. In Keith's poem it was the line "I still think of Taylor as if the wind is him." I mentioned how that line gives me such a feeling of the strong friendship between them and I like the way he connected the collecting of seeds in the wind with the memory of his friend. We talked about how much he must miss Taylor and discussed the possibility of sending him a copy of the poem in the mail. Keith was encouraged as a poet by the experience of writing his poem, but also by the response he received from his teacher and classmates. There were no red pen markings all over his poem; only sincere and heartfelt responses to words written honestly about a dear friend. Keith went on to write other poems, inspired, in part, by the supportive community of writers that surrounded him. His poem about Taylor became a reference point for future work and set a standard for other poems he wrote during the remainder of the school year. Whenever he shared a poem during a conference, for example, I asked him if he thought it had the same strength and honesty as his poem about Taylor. His response varied with each poem, and often his answer was to return to his writing to try to make it his best.

When a young poet knows his or her work will be received in the way Keith's poem was, there is a good chance that more poems will follow. The honest encouragement he or she feels will not only inspire more writing, but will often open the child up to receiving suggestions for improving the next poem. This isn't the case with every child, however. Although Keith's poem helped him grow as a writer, other children may listen in the moment and then proceed as if nothing was ever said. Part of the trust and respect that a teacher establishes has to include allowing children who aren't ready to make leaps as poets to grow in their own time. Like the gardener who watches over freshly sprouting plants bursting through the soil at different times, we have to keep in mind that young poets behave in much the same way. We have to keep watering and trusting, and eventually the poets and plants will bloom.

When children know their poetry is valued by others, through the example set by a thoughtful and trusting teacher, they, in turn, become more receptive to the efforts of their classmates. This kind of receptivity comes only after experiencing success and acceptance by a group of fellow poets who care and have learned to treat each other respectfully as writers and human beings.

The process of learning to work this way requires a shift in how we establish classrooms. It demands that we fill our schools with teachers who first and foremost respect children and their ideas. It necessitates setting aside time from mandated materials to allow poetry to blossom. For young poets to thrive, classrooms need different kinds of spaces for writing. Children need to be able to work quietly in private spaces or have the option of exchanging ideas with a fellow poet. Some need to sit at a table with other writers, while others prefer an isolated spot on the floor with soft pillows and a clipboard. I've even seen a few writers barricade themselves off from the rest of the class by building a structure with wooden blocks. One of the favorite writing places in our classroom recently has been a vacant space under a large storage shelf. What is important is that choices and options are available. Chapter 4 will examine specifically what we can do to maintain an optimum environment for young poets.

When the setting is right for poetry to thrive in a classroom—when good writing habits are modeled and writers feel supported in their work—there is a pervading sense of belonging. Young poets who feel encouraged by those around them feel valued as community members and will give back to the community willingly. When they know that their thinking and writing count, they will move forward with confidence in their lives as writers. The enthusiasm they feel for their own work, as well as for the work of their peers, will serve to continue the process. Like the water cycle which continually nurtures the very essence of life on our planet, the passion and caring felt by young writers who know their words are important will sustain the community which surrounds them. In turn, the well-established writing community will give each individual writer the courage and inspiration to keep going, to write the words hidden in the heartfelt places of our daily lives.

CHAPTER FOUR

Not a Day without Mud

I can still picture Chelsea with her red bowl, sitting quietly week after week, mushing her hands in that bowl of mud. Each week her mud would dry out and she'd repeat the same process. She'd fill the bowl with water and spend the next two hours stirring and kneading her mixture until it was just the right consistency. Beside her, Indra worked on her own project, a small wall she was constructing of mud. Each time we ventured out to the garden, she would add another layer to it, never deterred by rain or other adverse weather conditions that added their touch to her masterpiece.

In other parts of the garden, mud was the medium as well. A small group of children formed the Sun Devil Brick Company (named after Arizona State University's popular football team). They spent all of their time excavating mud out of a hole and then forming it into bricks and mud balls, but mostly getting it all over their clothes and themselves. When I commented to Erik about the quantity of mud on his pants, he said, "I know. You have to, it's lots messier than adobe."

While the Sun Devil Brick Company was busy creating their free-form mud products (and spending a large amount of time trying to establish who was in charge of the company), Kinley and Bryan took a more disciplined approach to mud. Following our adobe "inservice" with Bill, they made hundreds of miniature adobe blocks and stored them in cardboard boxes as they dried. Then they painstakingly assembled their blocks with adobe mortar they mixed up themselves. Over the course of several months, the walls of their model adobe houses grew straight and tall. Kinley added windows and inner walls. He brought in sod discarded from a neighbor's lawn renovation to give his house a bit of landscaping. Their concentration and perseverance were as solid as the walls they built.

In time, as the days of mud work accumulated, results of the children's efforts could be seen all over the garden. The mud from holes dug in one place became structures somewhere else. Mud walls reinforced by river rocks housed bees in the spring, opening up a whole new area of interest. The carefully constructed model houses reminded all who entered our outdoor space that the work going on was not to be taken lightly. It became evident that the children's play, which became serious work, transformed an empty garden plot into a living community. It was a metaphor in mud for the power of establishing a daily writing practice.

Encouraging young children to play with mud is one thing; bringing them along as poets is another. Nevertheless, our weekly mud encounters revealed insights that remain significant for me as a teacher and writer. One of Donald Murray's most emphatic points for writers is to get your rear end in the chair every day. This is hard enough for adults, but for seven-year-olds it's nearly impossible. Or rather, it's not so much getting to the chair, it's staying in it and keeping your body still enough to even begin to write. And then there's always the problem of forgetting your pencil, forgetting your daybook, realizing that your pencil isn't sharp enough, or sitting next to a friend who is infinitely more interesting than what's floating—or not floating—around in your mind. Throw in the added problem of not having anything to write about, and you're faced with a challenge. Establishing a writing practice to become a poet when you're in second grade is hard work. Being the teacher of second-grade poets is even harder work. Nevertheless, it can be done.

In our class we begin the journey as poets in a variety of ways. There are several pieces that fit together and happen at the same time. Each of the pieces will be described here briefly and then examined further in the following chapters. It is important to remember that although the individual aspects of poetry work can be viewed one at a time, they all work simultaneously to promote the writing of young poets.

Extending an Invitation to Other Poets

As teachers of young poets, we can't do it alone. We need the voices of other poets to help us find our way. We need to hear possibilities so we can make choices in the kinds of poems we want to write. I find it helpful, especially at the beginning of a school year, to read a variety of poems from well-known published poets.

I read playful rhyming poems from poets like Jack Prelutsky or Shel Silverstein that make everyone laugh. One of our favorites is Prelutsky's (1984) "Bleezer's Ice Cream Store," which includes lines like these:

> I am Ebenezer Bleezer,
> I run BLEEZER'S ICE CREAM STORE,
> here are flavors in my freezer
> you have never seen before,
> twenty-eight divine creations
> too delicious to resist,
> why not do yourself a favor,
> try the flavors on my list:
>
> COCOA MOCHA MACARONI
> TAPIOCA SMOKED BALONEY
> CHECKERBERRY CHEDDAR CHEW
> CHICKEN CHERRY HONEYDEW
> TUTTI-FRUTTI STEWED TOMATO
> TUNA TACO BAKED POTATO . . . (48)

I introduce them to the thoughtful, more reflective poetry of Mary Oliver, and to poems from Walt Whitman and Emily Dickinson that have been with us for a long time. I want them to experience a wide range of poems and poets so they can see many possibilities. As they begin to write their own lines, this introduction to different poets will expand their ideas of what they themselves can do.

I find it helpful for each child to have a personal anthology of poetry which we add to as the year progresses. We read from our anthology on a regular basis, and at the end of the school year each child then has a wonderful collection of poems by which to remember the year. Not every poem I read to my students ends up in the anthology, of course, but I do try to include their favorites, as well as ones I believe are important for them to be familiar with and to know.

Several years ago, Georgia Heard first introduced me to the idea of selecting a poem for each child. I do this now at the beginning of the school year, choosing a poem (or song) a week until each child has received one. I mount the poems on the wall along with the self-portraits the children draw on the first day of school. As the weeks of the new school year accumulate, one wall of our classroom fills with poems and portraits of familiar faces. I also add a copy of each poem to the class anthology. This collection is yet another way to remember the poetry we've shared and also those with whom we've shared it.

As part of this invitation of other poets into our class-room, it is vital to have a wide range of poetry books available to the children at all times. I have listed most of our classroom titles in the Recommended Works at the end of this book. I keep all of my poetry books together on a shelf where the children always have access to them. Additionally, I pull a smaller number of titles out and put them in tubs according to different categories for easier use. Some of the categories might be:

◆ poems in two languages
◆ funny poems
◆ rhyming poetry
◆ anthologies
◆ poems for two voices
◆ poetry written by other children
◆ holiday poetry
◆ animal poems
◆ poetry related to a particular content study

For example, during a study of human rights, we usually examine the writing of several African American poets. In that collection I might include the following titles:

Spin a Soft Black Song by Nikki Giovanni
Honey, I Love and Other Love Poems by Eloise Greenfield
Pass It On: African-American Poetry for Children by Wade
    Hudson
The Dream Keeper and Other Poems by Langston Hughes
This Same Sky: A Collection of Poems from around the World
    by Naomi Nye
*Children of Promise: African-American Literature and Art for
    Young People* edited by Charles Sullivan

I change the books in these tubs on a regular basis so my students will see a wide range of work from poets who, in time, become important members of our writing community. Their own poems often become part of the collections, too, as the school year progresses.

Let Child Poets Be Teachers

Over the years I've collected poems from my students, and I include anthologies of their work in my classroom alongside the volumes of published poets. I have also kept copies of individual poems on hand to use as examples. I use these during mini-lessons to give my students ideas and to reinforce the notion that children can be teachers as well. It is especially exciting for children to see the work of an older child they once knew in the school when they were younger. It is also an inspiration to them to know that their work might be used in the same way to teach other young poets someday. One day after I'd shown a previous student's work, Jesse wrote an exceptionally good poem. I told him I'd like to use it in the future to show other children how to write well. He replied, "I was hoping you'd say that." Later in his garden log he wrote: "Thanks for saying you would read my poem to other classes that I made today." When our students know we value their work enough to use it to instruct others, it elevates their confidence in themselves because it is yet another reminder of how much we trust and believe in them.

To Teach Poets We Must Be Poets

Although it is often risky to do so, I think it is important to share our own writing with our students. As I mentioned in Chapter 3, if we are asking them to reveal themselves through their poetry, it only seems fair that we do the same. I strongly believe that if we want to be proficient teachers of young poets, we have to practice what we are teaching. We need to know firsthand what it's like to struggle to find a topic, to find the line, to select the words which exactly express what is in our hearts. If we are asking children to take on these challenges, we need to do it, too. When our students see that we can be vulnerable and reveal ourselves, they are more likely to take the risk of exposing their innermost thoughts and feelings. Seeing our struggles helps them to trust the process and to trust their audience when sharing lines of poetry. Our personal example as poets will carry us a long way in inspiring our students as poets. When we share parts of ourselves with our students, it helps them know us better. They begin to see that we are humans just like they are, facing each day with the same questions and challenges they face. We are using writing to try to make sense of our own lives, too. They will continue to look to us for guidance and inspiration if they know that we're right beside them working through the same process. When they see it every day, it becomes an even more powerful experience for them and for us as their teachers.

Establish a Practice

One of the most important aspects of working with young poets is allowing time for the poetry to flourish. Time allows for patience and practice, two necessary components of a

strong poetry program. If we are always rushing our students
to finish their work in a short amount of time, we will never
get the quality of work that is potentially there. Poets cannot
be hurried and they need to trust that, as teachers, we'll give
them the time necessary to say what they want to say.

I find that an hour a day of writing in the classroom is
required to nurture young writers and poets. Throughout a
school year, that time isn't always devoted to poetry, but the
practice and the ritual established during such a writing
period certainly contribute to the development of emerging
poets. Writing each day begins with a brief mini-lesson (see
Chapter 5) and is followed by silent writing.

Silent writing is one of the most powerful aspects of our
classroom work as poets. I write in my daybook alongside the
children and it is a time when we are all equal. The children
see me modeling what I want them to do. We usually begin
with five minutes each day and gradually build up to twenty
minutes by the end of the school year. There are several basic
rules for silent writing:

◆   No talking.

◆   Stay in your chair.

◆   Keep writing. If you finish something, start a new piece.

◆   Don't interrupt the teacher, except in the case of an
    emergency.

The last rule is one of the hardest for young writers to follow.
They need reminders to keep writing. Sometimes they are so
excited about finishing a poem or story that they rush over to
share it with me. There are also a few children who think the
rules are for everybody else and choose to talk or interrupt
because they feel like it. I have found that if I'm really disciplined in the beginning about ignoring their interruptions
during silent writing, they tend to get the message and stop
doing it as frequently. To do this I simply continue concentrat-
ing on my writing and try to convey nonverbally that I'm busy
with my writing and they should be too.

In the past few years I have found it helpful to set a timer for silent writing. I wait until everyone is settled into their writing and then set it for the desired period of time. Doing this takes the responsibility of keeping track of the clock off of me, and I can concentrate on my own writing. Furthermore, it sends the message to the class that, again, I'm equally involved in my writing and don't wish to be distracted by anything or anyone during that time.

I have also begun using quiet music during this time. If I forget to put it on, invariably one of the children will ask for it. We use a variety of music, including classical, a wide range of music from around the world, and soft piano, guitar, or flute pieces. Music without recognizable lyrics seems to be the best for this part of our writing practice. I've noticed that the children stay more focused when the music playing is calm and relaxing. Somehow it serves as a reminder that this is a sacred time, not to be disturbed by talking and moving around. It helps them be more reflective and relaxes them into the day's writing. It seems to inspire them to take their writing more seriously. This may not work with all groups of children, but I've found it to be helpful with my young writers. Some of the music we use is listed in the Recommended Works section.

Sharing Our Lines

Immediately after silent writing the children usually line up to show me what they've done. Most young children are eager to share their work, and I try to read as much of their writing as quickly as I can. I do this for two reasons: One, so I can check each child's progress, and two, so I can see what we might need to work on in future mini-lessons or if there's exceptional writing that others would benefit from hearing.

I try to provide an opportunity to share as a whole group at the end of each writing period. If we're sharing poetry, usually everyone will have a chance. If there isn't enough time, for whatever reason, I sometimes set up small sharing groups of three or four so each child has a chance to share. This arrangement tends to shift throughout the year, depending on what we're doing with writing. It is important to remember to include sharing so the children can learn from each other. Sharing is a significant time to celebrate wonderful lines, and to point out when a young poet has given us a surprise by saying something in a new way.

Another way to share surprising lines is to make a wall chart either of lines found in published works or those taken from children's poems in the classroom. This can be an ongoing project with lines being added as they are discovered or written. It helps children become more aware of good writing, and it's yet another way for them to know their work is valued alongside the poetry of published poets.

As poems are written I try to make a copy for everyone to have and/or hang a copy on the wall for others to read. Once poetry gets going in a classroom, this is impossible to do with every poem written, but it's an especially important practice at the beginning of the year. Celebration of good work goes a long way when young poets are just getting started. As special anthologies are written (e.g., during the holiday season, in response to special class studies, etc.), I always make sure to send home the complete collection to be shared with parents and to add to the children's permanent poetry library at home. I have had parents say how much they appreciate this and that it has raised their awareness of poetry, often inspiring them to provide their child with more poetry in the home.

Poetry Every Day

Once we begin to include poetry in our everyday lives, it becomes a source of inspiration and enrichment for everything we do. It helps us make connections between what is in our hearts and what we experience through our daily living. Poetry helps us see the commonalities in our lives and reminds us we're not alone. I try to include poetry in my classroom that covers a wide range of the human experience.

Occasionally I ask parents and children to share their favorite poems from home. One year in honor of Mother's Day, I asked each mother in the class to send in her favorite poem either from childhood or as an adult. We read these in class and then wrote poems for our mothers. Both collections were assembled, duplicated, and given as Mother's Day gifts.

Another way I've encouraged parents to participate in our poetic lives is to send a poem home for homework to read and discuss with their child. One poem I sent for this kind of homework was Myra Cohn Livingston's "We Could Be Friends" (Janeczko 1990, 26):

We Could Be Friends

We could be friends
Like friends are supposed to be.
You, picking up the telephone
Calling me

    to come over and play
    or take a walk,
    finding a place
    to sit and talk,

Or just goof around
Like friends do,
Me, picking up the telephone
Calling you.

Teagan's response to the poem (Figure 4) is an example of this kind of work. By involving parents in our study of poetry, it not only draws them into what we are doing but sends a message to the child that poetry doesn't just have to be in school. It helps them see that poetry can be important to all of us at different stages of our lives and for different reasons. When I sent home the lyrics of Joni Mitchell's "The Circle Game," it stimulated discussions about the joys and the sorrows of experiencing a child grow up. The children also brought in stories of the song and how it had been a part of their parents' lives in years past. I don't send a poem home every week, but once in a while it's a good way to encourage dialogue and make connections. I have found that both parents and children enjoy this opportunity.

Another way in which I help children make poetry a part of their everyday lives is by introducing them to poems written about a wide variety of subjects. Certainly we read poems about feelings and the human experience, but I also like to share with them poems about the natural world, about the complexity of city life, and poems which teach us something about the creatures with whom we share our planet. I

Name teagan

Read the poem on the other side of this paper with someone in your family. Talk about it and write down a few thoughts or ideas you have about the poem. BONUS: Draw a picture about the poem.

this poem reminds me of Grace & me because we awaes (always) talk on the telephone, we have to talk on the telephone to stay friends Because Grace Lives faraway & goes to a difrint (different) school.

Sly cat

Sly Dog

Figure 4

can remember one child commenting, after reading one of Georgia Heard's animal poems from *Creatures of Earth, Sea, and Sky,* how interesting it was that it could be a poem and have information in it at the same time.

In addition to introducing children to this type of poetry, I believe it is equally important to ask them to write poems in response to a wide range of experiences and content. Some of the most powerful poetry written in my classroom has been in response to our study of human rights or to our biweekly visits to a nursing home. I have discovered that a poem often reveals more of what a child knows and understands in response to specific content than any other means of assessment. When we were about to end our year of work in the garden, we went outside with our daybooks and I asked the children to write a poem about their garden experience. Some of the poems simply described the kinds of activities that occurred during our time in the garden. Others, such as Denise's poem (Figure 5) revealed the profound influence of the experience on her life.

When I read Denise's poem and others that carried a similar appreciation for our year of outdoor days together, I was reminded what a powerful vehicle poetry is for self expression. I could have asked them to tell me what they thought about the garden or I could have requested that they fill out a survey to provide data for future curriculum decisions. I would have received factual information, but I wouldn't have seen into their hearts. Summarizing the garden experience through poetry gave me a glimpse into the depths of many of my students and showed me what mattered most to them. Writing a poem about such an important part of our year together revealed what had accumulated in the hearts of my students. Having the opportunity to express it through poetry allowed others to share it too. Like the houses Kinley and Bryan created from the individual adobe blocks they'd made, the poetry hidden in these young poets' hearts found a way to be expressed, thanks to the time we devoted to establishing a daily writing practice.

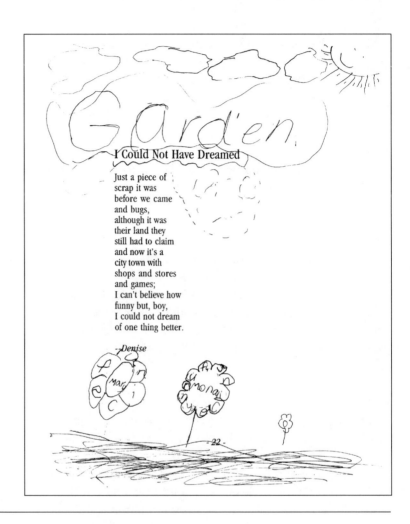

I Could Not Have Dreamed

Just a piece of
scrap it was
before we came
and bugs,
although it was
their land they
still had to claim
and now it's a
city town with
shops and stores
and games;
I can't believe how
funny but, boy,
I could not dream
of one thing better.

--Denise

Figure 5

Befriending the Geckos

During one of our first visits to the garden, Teagan discovered a beautiful gecko. I suggested that she leave it alone, but she persevered until she caught it. As she gently held it in her hand, she asked if she could keep it in a jar. I told her it would be better off if she let it go free. Michael overheard our conversation and said, "Put it up on the tree. I saw its wife up on the tree." Reluctantly she released the gecko back to its natural habitat.

In the weeks that followed, Teagan was on a mission to find her gecko again, whom she named Spike. She turned up every brick she saw and reminded her classmates to be careful as they searched for Spike. When a smaller gecko appeared in the marker container in our classroom one day, it was too much for Teagan. She began crying inconsolably, eventually telling me that the little gecko made her miss Spike. I suggested she might want to write a story about Spike to cheer herself up. She liked the idea and wrote a playful and entertaining story about Spike.

As the months went by, Teagan never found Spike. Yet he was as much a member of our garden community as anyone else. Teagan always had her eye open for him, and whenever anyone discovered even the slightest hint of a creature with a long tail, Teagan insisted it was Spike. Once when Kelly noticed something crawling into a brick where she was working, there was speculation that it might be Spike. Teagan was sure Spike had returned, and when she couldn't find him said, "Spike gets away with a lot of tricky things! That's the kind of brick he likes." Although Kelly insisted the creature she saw was much smaller than Spike, Teagan was certain that it was none other than her gecko.

Spike became somewhat of a legend in the garden, as well as a reference point for all other creatures. Not a brick, board, or stone was left undisturbed by Teagan in her pursuit of Spike. She explored all possibilities and never gave up her search for the gecko of her dreams. Teagan taught us all to keep our eyes wide open, to remain alert and ready for the treasures waiting to be discovered.

Teagan's quest for Spike is similar to what I do each day as a teacher of young poets. However, instead of searching for geckos, I'm always looking for ways to uncover the poems hidden away in interesting places of my students' lives. Like Teagan, turning over rocks, bricks, and boards, I am constantly seeking new possibilities for inspiring poetry writing in my classroom. One way this happens is through the mini-lessons I give from time to time. Some of them are specific to poetry writing, and others work for writing in general. The mini-lessons don't guarantee that poetry will be written, but as with Teagan in her search for Spike, they improve the odds just by virtue of the fact that we're paying more attention to what we're trying to do.

The mini-lessons I use have evolved over a number of years. They don't follow any particular sequence, although some naturally seem to come before others. Many have been borrowed and adapted from writers such as Georgia Heard, Ralph Fletcher, Don Murray, and Susan Stires. I am grateful to have had such good examples placed before me to guide my work with young poets.

Beginning

In addition to the ongoing poetry I read to my students, I often begin by talking about all of the different things about which a poem can be written. For example, a poem can be about a special shirt handed down from an older brother, a lost tooth, or a favorite animal. Rose's poem about a horse she rides serves as a good example (see Figure 6).

During early mini-lessons we talk about the wide range of subjects that can be included in a poem, as well as the various moods or feelings a poem can have. I show them playful poems such as Teagan's (Figure 7) or more reflective, wondering poems, like Kinley's (Figure 8). The more examples of poems they can see, the more they will be able to imagine writing possibilities for themselves. Even after they've begun

Figure 6

writing, it's important to keep showing them what is possible. Mary Oliver (1994) writes, "To write well it is entirely necessary to read widely and deeply. Good poems are the best teachers" (10).

Another early topic of discussion for poetry mini-lessons is the difference between a story and a poem. I usually begin by reading a poem that tells a story, such as William Stafford's "One Time" (Janeczko 1990, 58):

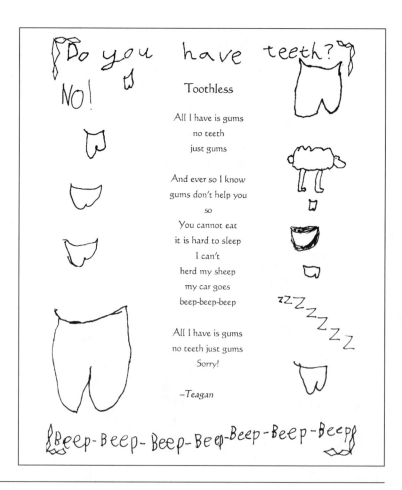

Figure 7

One Time

When evening had flowed between houses
and paused on the schoolground, I met
Hilary's blind little sister following
the gray smooth railing still warm from the sun
with her hand; and she stood by the edge
holding her face upward waiting
while the last light found her cheek
and her hair, and then on over the trees.

You could hear the great sprinkler arm
of water find and then leave the pavement,
and pigeons telling each other their dreams
or the dreams they would have. We were
deep in the well of shadow by then, and I
held out my hand, saying, "Tina, it's me—
Hilary says I should tell you it's dark,
and oh, Tina, it is. Together now—"

And I reached, our hands touched,
and we found our way home.

We talk about how a poem can tell a story but a story isn't
always a poem. Mary Oliver (1994) writes, "The first obvious
difference between prose and poetry is that prose is printed
(or written) within the confines of margins, while poetry is
written in lines that do not necessarily pay any attention to the
margins, especially the right margin" (35). Pointing out this
difference is an easy place for children to begin to understand
what separates poetry from a story.

A poem uses imagery in ways that prose does not. Poetry
leaves spaces for the reader to fill in his or her own meaning,
often by making comparisons between things. "A familiar
thing is linked to an unknown thing, as a key, to unlock the
mystery, or some part of the mystery, of the thing that is
unknown" (Oliver 1994, 99). Mary Oliver describes poetry as
a river where many voices travel and a latch that, when lifted,
gives us a glimpse into a greater paradise. When children are
just starting out as poets, conversations that include such
imagery enable them to lift the latch that releases the poetry
within them.

First-time poets and their parents often have it in their minds that a poem must rhyme. This kind of thinking is primarily due to the fact that most of us were taught to view poetry in this same limited way. Also, much of the mainstream poetry available to young children tends to rhyme (e.g., nursery rhymes, Dr. Seuss). As teachers, I believe it is important for us to introduce our students to the wonderful classic poetry which has withstood the test of time, as well as contemporary rhyming poets like Prelutsky and Shel Silverstein.

Figure 8

But it is also important to help them see early on in their career as poets that free verse can be equally playful, inspiring, and well crafted. I have found that very young poets who try to write rhyming verse often sacrifice any kind of meaning or sense making for the sake of the rhyme. They write things like "The man ran and ran and he carried a tan fan." When they are older, some do well with rhyming verse, and occasionally a young child will come along who has a talent for rhymes. However, most children appear to do better with the freedom and flexibility of free verse when they are just starting out.

Getting Ideas for Poems

I have found that one of the most important mini-lessons, especially early in the year, is teaching children how to get ideas for poems. Certainly they will find inspiration in the poetry we read to them, and there are other ways to spark ideas as well. This is one of the times I try to use several examples of work from other children. One of my favorite examples is this poem written by Celina about her father:

> Crazy Father
>
> her crazy father nags and nags
> and makes her dance
> on the coffee table
> and makes her start every sentence
> with the word "so"
> and he also makes mashed potatoes
> with every dinner
> and he made the White House
> out of mashed potatoes
> tomorrow night we're having
> the Statue of Liberty
>
> well,
> so what if he makes her dance
> on the coffee table
> well,

so what if he makes weird dinners
with mashed potatoes
like the White House and the Statue of Liberty
well, it doesn't matter
because she loves him

After Celina wrote this poem, she told me she got the idea about the coffee table and starting each sentence with "so" from Patricia MacLachlan's book *Baby*. The mashed potatoes came from a Doritos commercial on TV. The love, I am certain, came from her relationship with her father.

Helping young children find topics for their poems that they care deeply about takes time and patience. For most children it takes more than one mini-lesson. I see this as an ongoing process which continues throughout an entire school year. When the proper attention is given to this aspect of poetry writing, there can be wonderful results. One of my most memorable examples was six-year-old Andréa, just starting out her career as a poet. As we were beginning to write our first lines of the year, she came to me and said, "My head is empty without any poems." In a very short time she wrote a playful poem about her littlest finger and included the lines "My pinky is very brown like/hot chocolate or/rose-wood." She became one of the strongest poets in our class and at the end of second grade published her first collection of poems about a variety of important topics in her life.

Line Breaks

When first starting out as poets, most children have little experience with the concept of line breaks. They write the words of their poems straight across the page, filling in a whole line before moving to the next one. Again, showing them a variety of examples seems to be the best way to teach the idea of line breaks. I tell my students that the decision of where to put in a line break is a personal choice and each poet has the right to decide where line breaks should go. We talk about how line breaks remind the reader of a poem to pause for a moment before reading the next line. Sometimes I'll take a poem I've written (or a poem by any other poet) and write the lines straight across the page (Figure 9). I'll read each line, stopping only at the end of the line for a breath. Children easily begin to see that a poem arranged this way not only doesn't look like a poem, but doesn't sound like one either. Then I show them how to put a slash between words where they think a line break should be (wherever I've naturally paused to take a breath or to read it so that it sounds like a poem). Later I show them what the same poem looks like with the line breaks included (Figure 10). We talk about how the placement of line breaks can change the meaning of a poem. Line breaks can stretch out a poem and give it space. One of my favorite examples of this is Narcissa's poem about the chili pepper lights their family hangs up at Christmas time (Figure 11).

Saying Something in a New Way

One observation I've made over the years of working with young poets is their inclination to use words that have gone stale (Heard 1989). We call them tired words. I usually handle this mini-lesson by compiling a list of words on a large piece of chart paper. We do this as a whole group and add to it over the course of the year. A few of the regulars on the tired word chart are *nice, pretty, fun, bad, good, exciting, big, little, mad,* etc. Sometimes it takes the children awhile to realize that words on this list need to be adjectives. Some will offer words like *the, and, of, with,* etc., and we then have to discuss the different kinds of words that make up our language. This is often a natural time to present mini-lessons about nouns, verbs, adjectives, adverbs, and prepositions, depending on the age of the children.

One of the most significant related mini-lessons is one focusing on saying something in a new way. I was first intro- duced to this idea by Georgia Heard, and it makes such sense

There are moments when I know / I should pay attention / for a poem and a lesson have arrived / When I saw those tiny fingers / reaching out like miniature tweezers / to grasp each parade of bubbles / my eyes opened wider / and I listened with more than my ears

Figure 9

A Lesson from Bubbles 12/2/93

There are moments when I know
I should pay attention
For a poem and a lesson have arrived

When I saw those tiny fingers
Reaching out like miniature tweezers
To grasp each parade of bubbles
My eyes opened wider
And I listened with more than my ears

As the round prisms of color
Shimmered in the late afternoon light
Words and images appeared as well

What I learned—enjoy each moment
As fleeting as it may be
For even after it has disappeared
The joy and laughter will linger
For as long as they're invited to remain

Figure 10

in helping young writers develop as poets. She demonstrated
a process that has been invaluable in my own classroom work
with poetry and especially in helping children expand their
use of poetic language. I first do this as a whole group using
large chart paper, just as I do with the list of tired words. What
Georgia has suggested is to describe an event or idea in
regular words, listing what we know about it on one half of
the page. Drawing a line down the middle, on the other half
of the paper we take each line on the list and think of a new

chili pepper lights

by Narcissa

we
hang
up
the
red
bright
chili pepper
lights
they
light
up
the
whole
house
a bright
red
like
roses
in
our
back
yard

Figure 11

way to say it. This class poem about Halloween demonstrates
the process:

◆ you get lots of candy by going to   Baskets overflow from the top
   many houses   with mouth-watering yum-nums

◆ you trick-or-treat and get lots of   Every corner you turn
   candy   Everywhere you look
◆ when you go trick-or-treating you   Everywhere you spy from the
   wear coctumes   corner of your eye
                                                       are cartoon characters
◆ some people put real and fake   creepy, crawly, icky monsters
   cobwebs up for decorations   princesses from around the world
                                                       angels flown down from the sky

◆ pumpkins, pumpkins are
   everywhere at every door

                                                       At every door pumpkins, pumpkins
                                                       teeny and humongous

◆ spooks like ghosts and goblins
   represent Halloween   That's Halloween!

◆ skeletons are hung up by your
   doorway to make it spooky
◆ some people dress up like witches
   and cowboys and cowgirls

     Some children grasp this idea easily and apply it to their
writing immediately. Others need more time and practice
before being able to think and write "in a new way." After
going through the whole class exercise, I find it helpful to
show many examples of children's poetry that demonstrates
saying something in a new way. Jesse's poem (Figure 12)
about his dog that died is one of the best examples I've seen.
     Jesse's line "the dog whose heart went blank" was
astonishing to me. I asked him how he got the idea to write it
and he said, "I didn't want to just say 'my dog died', so I tried
to think of a new way to say it." Later as he was working on
the last section, he again included two lines which were most
unusual. To describe himself crying he wrote "his boy's eyes
were clear like water in a lightbulb shape." And to express the

heartache he felt at the loss of his dog he used the phrase "my heart sliced in half." At the age of eight, Jesse is already one of those rare young poets who innately understands how to use words in powerful ways to create poetry. Children like Jesse can do wonders in bringing others along with their writing. A child who can write this way knows how to break through the conventions of everyday language and find new and amazing ways to express a thought. When we have students like Jesse who naturally think poetically, it is essential that we highlight

Figure 12

their work for others to see and learn from. Young poets like
Jesse become strong teachers for all of us and show us a way
into unexplored territory with words. Our job as teachers is to
point out this exceptional use of language and let it guide us.

Choosing a Title

Many young writers have a tendency to tell their whole story
or poem in the title, for example, "The Time My Family Went
to Disneyland" or "When My Dog Ran Away and We
Couldn't Find Him for Three Days." In conjunction with our
discussions about saying something in a new way, we specifically talk about choosing a good title for a poem. I often tell
my students that in choosing a title for a poem, a good writer
tries to grab the readers' attention and not tell them everything
right away. We want to select a title that will make our readers
keep reading.

One of the first suggestions I make is to wait until the
poem is written before giving it a title. Often a strong line or
metaphor (see Chapter 7) will jump out that would be a
perfect title. I have used this poem from my own writing to
demonstrate this idea:

> Moon Face
> for Kelly
>
> On the day after what would have been
> Your sister's fourth birthday
> I find myself now strolling
> You around the familiar neighborhood where
> One magical evening I gave her the word "moon"
>
> I have stayed away from these quiet streets
> As long as I could for the memories
> Inspired by birdsongs, cacti, and silent sunsets
> Were more than I could bear
>
> Yet today we are together as the sun
> Finds its way out from behind the clouds
> And I notice your round face smiling up at me saying
> It's okay—you can love me, too

When I shared this poem with my students, I explained it wasn't until I was well into writing the poem that I realized the connection between the word *moon* I taught Kelly's sister, and Kelly's own moon-shaped face. Once this association was made, I knew what the title of my poem would be.

There are times, however, when a title comes to mind first, and the poem comes later. When my granddaughter fell asleep in my arms as I walked along the beach in Hawaii last summer, the title "Beach Lullaby" popped into my head. I wanted to write a poem that described the calming effect of the waves, almost like a cradle rocking. This is the poem that followed:

> Beach Lullaby
> for Zoë
>
> At the shoreline's far end where
> black lava rocks halted the white sand
> I traded my plastic bag of beach glass
> for a wide-eyed baby
> handed over by her mommy
> whose arms were weary for the moment
>
> We began our stroll back along the water's edge
> as tie-dyed clouds turned dusk to pink
> our gazes drawn out to the Pacific
> one talking, one listening
> both mesmerized by the ocean's breathing
>
> Conversation soon gave way
> to silence as the girl child napped in my arms
> drooling and breathing
> an ocean treasure yet to be tossed about
> by the sandy waves of time

It is also helpful to have the whole class help select a title for a poem. We do this for both stories and poems. One time I told my class a story about an incident that happened when I was four, the first day I went to preschool. As it turned out, a girl's arm became stuck in the wooden chair and the custodian had to saw the chair apart to get her arm out. The class helped generate this list of possible titles for my story:

My First Day of Preschool
Oh, No!
The First Day of School
Stuck In Preschool
Uh-oh!
Arm Stuck in the Chair
Stuck Tight
Chair Stuck
Trouble
I'm Nervous about Going to Preschool

After writing all suggestions on a large piece of chart paper, we looked them over carefully and voted on the one we thought would make a reader want to keep reading. "Stuck in Preschool" won almost unanimously, especially after we discussed the way the word *stuck* was used and how it carried a dual meaning. Later in the year we used this experience as a reference point for choosing poetry titles. Some children used this strategy independently, while others didn't. The children who understand puns and multiple layers of meaning tend to apply the strategy more frequently, both in their own work and as suggestions to peers during editing conferences.

After this mini-lesson about title selection was presented, many more children chose intriguing titles for their poems, wholeheartedly interested in maintaining their readers' attention. Others kept right on giving the summary of their poem in its title, not really caring what anyone thought. Gradually, though, most of them began to see that finding a good title for a poem was an important part of the process, and they came to enjoy their audience's response to their clever and innovative poem titles.

Line Repetition

In our class we often talk about the way certain poems are tied together, either through a line that connects the beginning and the end, or a line repeated throughout the poem. When children are just starting out as poets, it is common for them to write one short verse and declare that the poem is finished. When I confer with a child who has done this, I often say that it seems as if there is more to the poem than what is on the page, that the poem is just getting started and it's already over. One suggestion I offer to help him or her extend the poem is to pick a line that stands out in the first verse and incorporate it in some way later on in the poem. Nathan's poem about his lost tooth is a good example of a poem that ties the beginning and the end together by repeating the same line (Figure 13).

Like A Penny Only Smaller

My tooth
is loose, it's small
It's looser
every day
    It's like a penny
    only smaller
It fell out
I have a big space in
my mouth
    It's like a penny
    only smaller

--Nathan

Figure 13

When Nathan originally wrote his poem, he had only written the first six lines. As we talked about it, he added in conversation: "It fell out/I have a big space in/my mouth." I suggested he write that down, and then we talked about the possibility of repeating the lines "It's like a penny/only smaller." Pleased with the revisions, Nathan made an easy decision to give his poem the title "Like a Penny Only Smaller."

Andréa's poem, "Through the Tangled Roses" (Figure 14), uses line repetition in a slightly different way. She uses the line "Through the tangled roses" at the beginning of each of her first three stanzas and then slightly alters it at the end of her poem. Using repetition in this way gives her readers a sense of the garden's intensity with its tangles of plant life, and then allows them to step back a bit and simply appreciate the beauty of the flowers as they pass through her garden. Andréa wrote her poem entirely independent of any teacher assistance. It is a strong example of how children naturally inter-

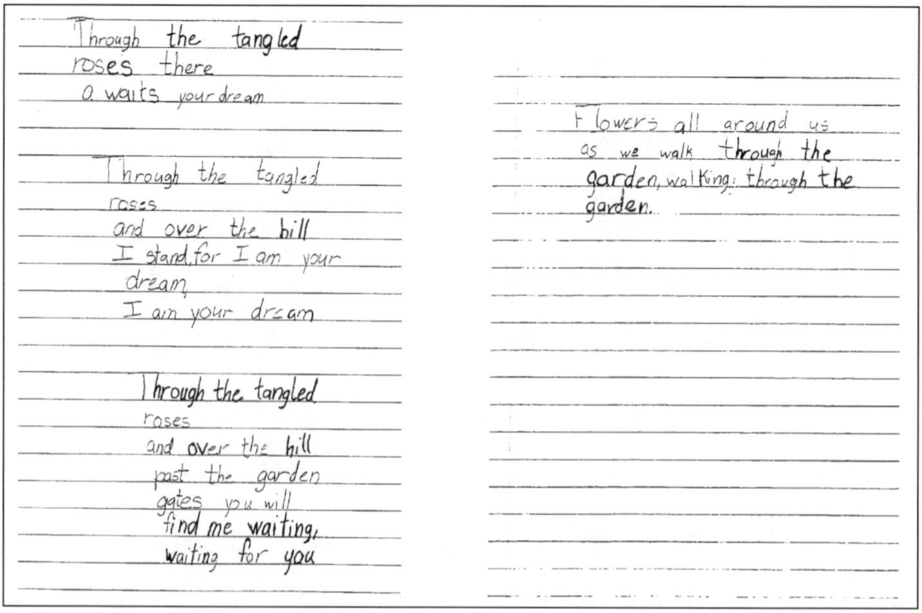

Through the tangled
roses there
awaits your dream

Through the tangled
roses
and over the hill
I stand, for I am your
dream
I am your dream

Through the tangled
roses
and over the hill
past the garden
gates you will
find me waiting,
waiting for you

Flowers all around us
as we walk through the
garden, walking through the
garden.

Figure 14

nalize the idea of line repetition if they are given enough experiences with it. Once line repetition is introduced to young poets, they begin to see it around them everywhere. They see lines repeated in songs they sing and in the work of published poets. With practice they learn to use line repetition to effectively shape the direction of their own verse, just as Nathan and Andréa have done.

Showing versus Telling

A challenge I have found in helping young children become poets is getting them to paint an image with words, rather than just telling about an event or idea. It's somewhat like the process of choosing a title: spaces need to be left for readers to fill in the blanks with their own meanings and understandings. One of my favorite examples of showing versus telling is a letter written by Richie to his friend Cynthia who was transferring to another school. Although it was a letter rather than a poem, the language is poetic and demonstrates how a deeper, more descriptive picture of a relationship can be presented by showing rather than telling (Figure 15).

When I use this letter as an example of showing versus telling, I point out to my students the way in which Richie managed to let Cynthia know how much he cared for her and how much he would miss her without ever using those words. By using lines such as "I liked . . . how you're so good at being cats/no matter how wild or tame," he described what was important in his relationship with her and let us all have a view of the delightful friendship they had established, without saying it directly. This is the kind of descriptive language I try to inspire my students to use in their poems. It's also a good reminder that poetry doesn't have to be limited to poems--it can be found in letters, brochures, conversations between friends, and in the stories we write and tell each day. When we, as teachers, make an effort to point out these poetic lines to our students, they will eventually begin to do it on their own in the poems they write themselves.

In addition to showing my students writing like Richie's, I often have them do some exercises for homework, especially at the beginning of the year, which encourage them to look at a specific subject with more detail. This can be done in a variety of ways, and each year I do it a bit differently, depending on my group of students. One of the first assignments I give them is to think of a memory of when they were little. I encourage them to think of something specific and include sounds, visual images, and feelings. Mikey's poem "I Restore"

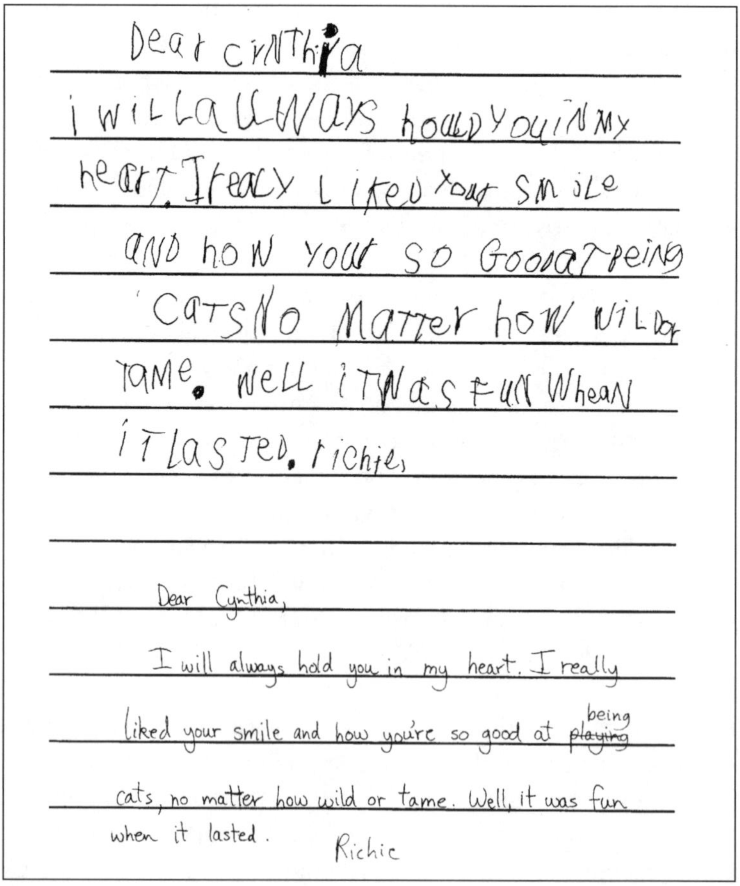

Dear Cynthia,

I will always hold you in my heart. I really liked your smile and how you're so good at being cats, no matter how wild or tame. Well, it was fun when it lasted.

Richie

Figure 15

(Figure 16) is a playful poem about playing with the lids in his mom's kitchen when he was a baby.

Sometimes I'll ask my students to make a list of images. This won't be a poem yet, but it holds the potential to be transformed into one. During our ocean study I asked everyone to make a list of images of the sea. I gave them an example from my own experience on the coast of Maine: herons tugging eels out of the mud at low tide. Here are a few of the images children wrote down:

◆　A dragon with the longest tail and eyes that cross

◆　A sea otter slinging its tail

I Restore

I remember
when I was two
I played with pots.
Drummy-drummy, yeah!
Drummy-drummy, yeah!
Does this top go on this pot?
Yeah!
It does!

--Mikey

Figure 16

◆   Starfish standing and looking like they don't know where
    they are
◆   Waves nervously coming up and down
◆   Lonely sailboats floating across the water

When it is time to share lines like these, I try to point out word
combinations that are surprising, such as "nervous waves"
and "lonely sailboats." It is helpful to make a large chart of
lines like these and add to it as more are discovered.

Another homework assignment I give to encourage
showing versus telling is to choose an ordinary item around
the house and make a list of details that describe it. I emphasize that this is not a poem, but lines from it could potentially
become a poem. Brian's list demonstrates this exercise (Figure
17).

What I found interesting about Brian's list was that he
matter-of-factly listed all the details about his new Suburban
and then at the end, almost as an afterthought, added, "My
mom smiles when she's in it." When Brian shared his list with
the class, I asked everyone if there were any surprising lines.
Several children mentioned the line about his mom, and we
talked about how that line could be the seed for a poem if
Brian chose to write about his new family car.

I'm not suggesting that we always give our students
exercises to help generate poetry. At some point we want
them to be able to think for themselves and to find inspiration
in their own ways. However, when they are just starting out, I
think helping them uncover a few stones where their poems
might be hiding—like in Teagan's search for her mythical
gecko—can be quite worthwhile. If they are led to possibilities, they will create their own.

Different Kinds of Poems

In thinking of possibilities for poetry, children need to know
that there are numerous types of poems from which to
choose, as well as subjects. They usually know the difference

between rhyming and free verse poetry, but there are other kinds that can be added to their list of alternatives. A few of the types I present to my students are:

◆ Information Poems—factual information in poetic form

◆ Question Poems—poems that include questions and leave you wondering

◆ Shape Poems—poetry with words arranged in interesting ways that are often tied to the poem's meaning

◆ Poems with different moods—happy, sad, reflective, silly, playful, etc.

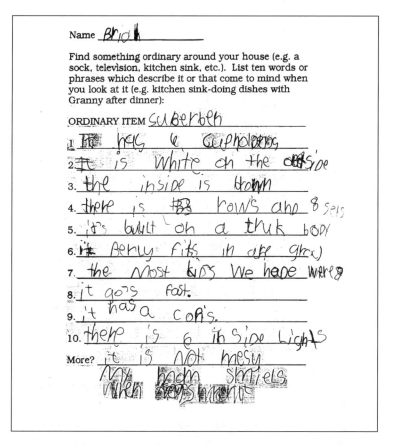

Figure 17

◆ Poems that tell a story—a story told in poetic form (see William Stafford's poem in previous section on Beginning)

◆ Poems for two voices—poetry written in two parts with the intention of being read by two people

In our class we often define an information poem as one that teaches us something in poetic form. Information poems teach us facts about nature or the world as well as give us images or thoughts to ponder. Many of the animal poems in Georgia Heard's *Creatures of Earth, Sea, and Sky* (1992) mentioned earlier are information poems. Her poem "Will We Ever See?" is a good example:

> Will We Ever See?
>
> Will we ever see a tiger again?
> stalking its prey with shining eyes?
>
> Will we see the giant orangutan
> inspecting its mate for fleas?
>
> Or a California condor
> feeding on the side of a hill?
>
> Or a whooping crane
> walking softly through a salty marsh?
>
> Or hear the last of the blue whales
> singing its sad song under the deep water?

"Will We Ever See?" is also a question poem. When we talk about question poems, we emphasize how they make us wonder. Question poems, like Kelly's (Figure 18), inspire us to ask more questions and to seek understanding of the issues raised. Question poems don't always have answers, but they help us see that many of us are pondering the same ideas. They stimulate conversation and keep us thinking and reflecting about our lives.

Shape poems are fun to make, and they often appear in the final draft stage after the poem's content has been determined. I've had some students, though, who started off with their poem in a special shape and adjusted the word selection according to the shape. There are some good examples of shape poems in X. J. and Dorothy Kennedy's *Knock at a Star: A Child's Introduction to Poetry* (1982) such as "Concrete Cat" by Dorthi Charles (Figure 19). While I don't require my students to write shape poems, it can be an enjoyable way to design a poem with interesting visual results. Young children like to guess what a shape poem is about before it is read to them. If you're into displaying your students' work on the walls, shape poems work really well for this.

Demonstrating different mood poems is one of the easiest mini-lessons to present. I use children's writing from my own classes and also the work of published poets. An

Figure 18

excellent book I've discovered recently is *Ten-Second Rainshowers* by Sandford Lyne (1996). It's a collection of poems written by children published in a beautifully illustrated book. The poems are divided into categories, one of which is feelings and moods. "My Friend" is from the section on challenges:

> My Friend
>
> I remember a girl
> named Jeanine.
> She was one of my friends.
> One day at school,
> they told us she had cancer.
> A week later they said
> she was dead.
> She's like a plant that
> I forgot to water.
>
> —Jessica Surrat, grade 6

The poems are generally short in length, and they work well with younger poets. Exposing children to poetry with a wide range of moods is, in my opinion, the best way to help them realize possibilities for themselves. When they are familiar

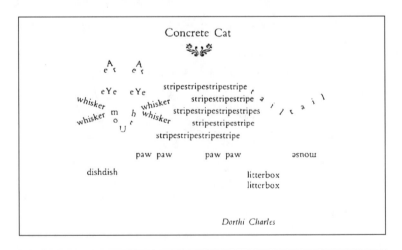

Figure 19

with the different moods of poems, they are more likely to explore them in their own writing. For example, in Chapter 3, Keith's poem about missing his friend Taylor is somewhat sad and reflective. This later poem, written around the theme of love, is serious but includes a humorous twist at the end (Figure 20).

Earlier in the chapter when I was explaining how we begin our work as poets, I mentioned that we talk about the difference between a story and a poem. Although this is presented during the introductory phase of poetry writing, I find it important to include mini-lessons throughout the year which focus on poems that tell a story. There are many wonderful story poems in *Ten-Second Rainshowers*, and I also share examples from my own students, such as Michelle's poem (Figure 21) about a friend's experience being the first African American to integrate an all-white school in the 1960s. As with all other kinds of poems, the more children

---

Love

**Love is weird but
people should thank
love
when men meet ladies
they want to get married
teenagers don't get married
they hang out**

by Keith

Figure 20

see and hear, the more they'll get the idea of how to write poems that tell stories.

I've had very few students write poems for two voices, but we do enjoy reading them. Perhaps if I placed more emphasis on this kind of poem I'd see more two-voice poems written in my classroom. Paul Fleischman has written many poems for more than one voice, and they are especially good for choral reading (see Recommended Works: General Children's Poetry Books). I try to include several two-voice poems in our class anthology to read and share. It's important for children to see what a poem for two voices looks like, as

But She Kept On Going

Elsie
The wonderful Elsie
She kept on going
Went to the grocery store
Held hands with a little white girl
Got in trouble
And didn't know what she did
But she kept on going

With the work of Dr. King
The schools would let African-Americans
Come into their schools
Nobody wanted to go but Elsie
When studying got pelted with chalk
But she kept on going

In the cafeteria was too quiet
So she knew something was going on
Got hit with mashed potatoes
Baby peas
Whatever kind of food you can think of
But she kept on going

Her stories were important
I won't forget her
She wouldn't let the hard times
Bother her
She takes time from her busy life
For children like us
And she keeps on going
Elsie

--Michelle

Figure 21

well as to hear it. As with other types of poems, the more children experience poems for two voices, the more they'll begin writing them.

Something Small That's Really about Something Big

As young writers begin to find their way as poets, they can be introduced to more sophisticated aspects of poetry. Once poetry writing is somewhat established in my classroom, I like to give a mini-lesson about poems written about something small that are really about something much bigger. I share this poem I wrote a few years ago about a cloth angel I made as a Christmas ornament for a little girl I knew and loved. It was written the night we were told she relapsed and her cancer was terminal:

> Christmas Angel
>
> The night they told me
> she was dying
> all I could think of
> was the golden-haired angel
> I made for her
> to hang on the tree
> in honor of baby's first Christmas.
>
> Throughout that sleepless
> night I kept seeing
> her angel
> dressed in cloth
> left over from the quilt
> I sewed for her
> in the mountains
> the summer before she was born.
>
> Soon she'll be leaving us. Her angel
> will stay behind to dance
> alone among the pine needles

each Christmas
reminding us of her,

the other angel called away
for her own dance
who departed entirely too soon.

I ask my students what they think the poem is about. Usually after seeing multiple examples of this kind of a poem they begin to understand how a poem written about something small can really be about something big. It is easy for them to see that my poem is about the cloth angel on the tree, but it's also about something much bigger—my love and feelings of loss for the little girl.

For many children, this kind of poem is beyond their developmental level, and it will be years before they can write a poem using symbolism or metaphor in this way. Yet I believe it is important to put these ideas out to children and see where they go with them. If we don't try to stretch them as writers, we may miss out on some amazing poetry. I think young writers are often underestimated, and this is an aspect of poetry writing where this occurs. When we believe they will write at such sophisticated levels, they will figure out a way to do so. Jesse's poem "The Feel of Them" (see Figure 12, page 57) demonstrates this very idea. It is true also with simile and metaphor.

Simile and Metaphor

The use of simile and metaphor ties in with many of the previously mentioned mini-lessons. It has to do with learning to say things in a new way and often to write about something small that is actually about something much larger. Chapter 7 is devoted entirely to an exploration of the use of simile and metaphor with young poets, so the mini-lessons I have used will be included there.

As we develop as poetry teachers, it is important to remember that our work is not to fill empty minds with

techniques and information, but to inspire and offer possibilities. When Teagan spent her year in search of her beloved
Spike, she never stopped looking and thinking of potential
spots where he might be hiding. If a new idea popped into her
head, she'd run with it until she was satisfied that he was
indeed not there. Teaching poetry writing is somewhat like
Teagan's search—when we have ideas we need to trust and
follow them. The mini-lessons I have included are not prescriptions for anyone to follow. They are simply presented as
possibilities, glimpses into the places I've taken children (and
they've taken me) in our efforts to uncover the poetry of their
lives.

Voices from the Earth

Voices carried the very essence of life in the garden. On a given day it was not surprising to hear the voices of two children arguing over a section of discarded chicken wire just inches away from several others happily chattering about the consistency of mud they were using to make miniature animals. Voices pleaded when a deal was to be made or shouted out in anticipation of a sale of some commodity. Voices convinced, sang, comforted, and created a reality that only those of us who were there understood. Voices revealed who we were individually and collectively.

One day when the Sun Devil Brick Company was going strong, I observed this conversation between several children who were mixing pots of mud:

Erik: Look at her pot of mud! Denise, you got all the rocks out. You're great for the company! [Erik continues sifting sand.] You gotta tell me how to make this. You gotta!

Denise: I'm not telling anyone how to do this!

Mikey: You gotta!

Denise: I won't but I'll make some for other people.

Mikey: For me?

Denise: It takes two months to dry!

Erik: For me? I will not spy!

Keith: [sitting on the periphery of the discussion] Don't trust him.

Erik: Ask Kelly if she's working for the company.

Kelly: Sure!

Mary: Am I in your way?

Denise: How could you be? You're the teacher! If you were, we'd
call you the way teacher!

The children's spirited enthusiasm for their work as brick makers
came through clearly in their voices, as did their appreciation for
Denise's good mixture and her passion to keep her recipe top secret.
Their voices revealed where they were relative to their own agendas
and to those of others surrounding them.
 Their voices from the garden also came through in the classroom. Each week they kept a log of their garden work and recorded
their activities. Many of them also took the liberty of adding their
own twist to their weekly garden summaries. Mikey's two log entries
revealed his voice and playfulness in a clear, entertaining way
(Figures 22a and 22b). His writing was an extension of his delightful personality.
 The personality of the community was equally well expressed
through The Garden News, a publication spontaneously written by

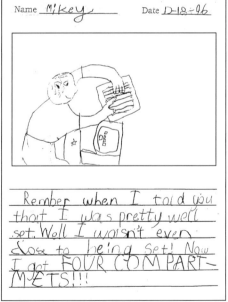

Name __Mik___ Date __9-25-9ð__

I'm Planing to put notes
and studypapers in my
compartment in my table.
I'v got alot done. I'v
got a nice desk a chair
I gese you can say I'm
prety set.

Name __Mikey__ Date __12-18-96__

Rember when I told you
that I was pretty well
set. Well I wasn't even
close to being set! Now
I got FOUR COMPART-
MENTS!!!

Figure 22a & 22b

several children (Figure 23). It contained a bit of nearly everything and everyone in its informative and comical reporting of the news. It was yet another reminder that the voice of our class and its garden community was alive and well.

Finding your voice as a writer is like falling in love. When you find your true voice, you know it's the real thing. It is exhilarating to experience that moment when what you are trying to say takes on a resonance of truth. You know there is a perfect balance between what is in your

GARDEN NEWS NOV. 20
By Teagan 1996 tasha

Andréa ,Indra,Chelsea & Caitlin have a new co. called the four girls river & brick co.

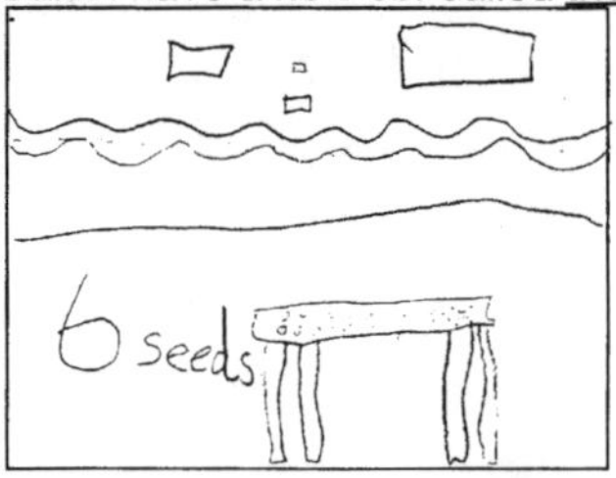

Anita,Kelly & Brian are bankers & they will give you six seeds if you put your seeds in the bank.

6 seeds

Garden cartoon.
comics are blasting out. more and more dumb bunnies. like #1 one bunny left. here comes America's funniest commedians Keith & Oliver.

News
Oliver,Keith,Erik & Sean are still geniuses. Teagan,Jesse, Eirk,Mikey & Oliver are runing president of rockey mountain. The vote is on tuesday. there's a New adobe & river co. in town. It is called the four girls river and brick co. it makes rivers & adobe bricks. what a adobe week.

Garden sports
Not much but there mhight be a Adobe fhight!

garden with Leigh
Leigh is selling rocks. Brian is fixing the bank.you get seeds if you're pore. Teagan is the new vet thacks to tasha. sick pet call
Natasha is still giving Jobs to Everbody. ten seeds for a job.

Figure 23

heart and what is appearing before you on the page. There is a clear connection between the writer and what is being written.

This is not an easy concept to teach young poets for many reasons. For one thing, they are not old enough to know what it's like to fall in love. They haven't written enough to experiment with different voices or to even know how different voices might sound. They are not experienced enough as writers or as human beings. Yet it is possible with much patience, and through work similar to that which I have previously mentioned, to help children find their voice as poets. One of the first things we have to do, and help our students do, is get comfortable with who we are.

Certainly all of the factors I've already mentioned contribute to helping young writers feel at ease and comfortable. A safe environment in which to write, a vigilant teacher, a wealth of examples, and practice all help writers become more proficient at their craft. For some children, finding one's voice is something that naturally emerges from all of these. Andréa is one of those children who, surrounded by a community of poets, found her voice primarily on her own. Her poem "Writing" (Figure 24) shows her comfort with words and enjoyment of the writing process. She has managed to express her love for writing in a way that is genuine, somewhat playful, and completely true to herself and her own voice. As I read her words I can picture her face with its radiant smile looking at me, knowing that I know what she has written is exactly what was in her heart.

Other children require a bit more time and effort to find their voices. One of the first challenges is helping them see that what they have to say matters and that readers are interested in what their voice has to say. This happens differently for individual children. Some poets, like Adam, thrive on public encouragement. At the beginning of the year, Adam wrote several pieces, just a few lines mostly, that had the feel of poetry but weren't fully developed. He loved any opportunity to share his writing with the entire class, and one day I noticed he had written about ravens more than once:

Who are you?
Who are you? Are you a raven
No, I am a man.

Listen
listen I will
make a raven
for you, okay?

Raven
Ravens are swift as the night

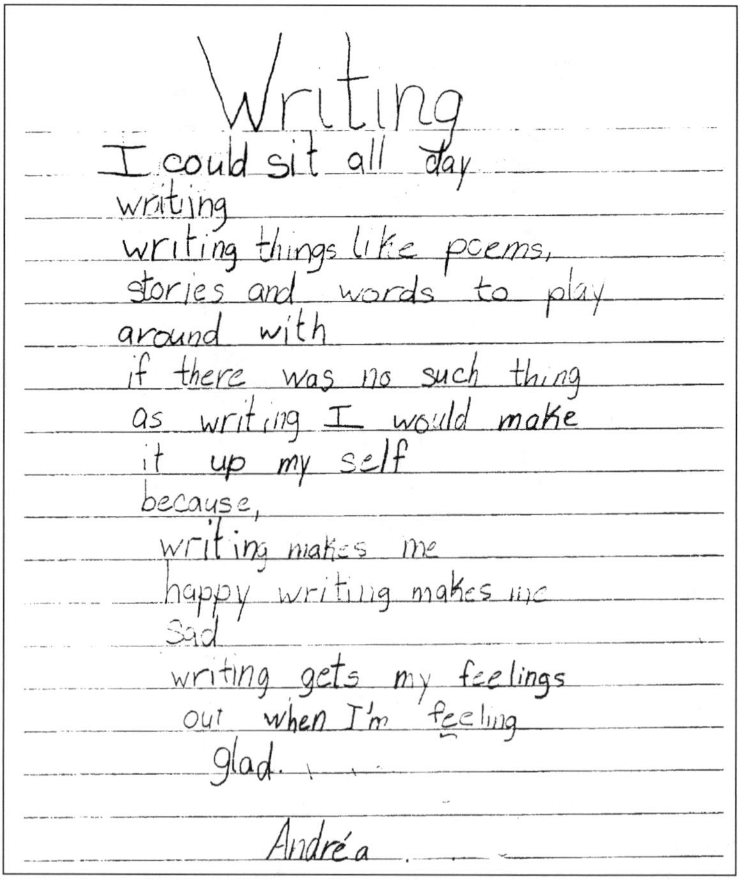

Writing

I could sit all day
writing
writing things like poems,
stories and words to play
around with
if there was no such thing
as writing I would make
it up my self
because,
writing makes me
happy writing makes me
Sad
writing gets my feelings
out when I'm feeling
glad.

Andréa

Figure 24

I asked if he'd be interested in taking the author's chair to read the few lines he'd written about ravens. He did this eagerly, and afterward I commented that it seemed like he was interested in ravens and knew a lot about them. I invited Adam to make a list of images or pictures that came to his mind when he thought of ravens. Soon after my invitation was issued, he wrote this poem:

> The Raven
>
> The raven flies
> right through the
> door its wing
> so keen
> all night

Adam didn't stick with the raven theme after that, but when it came time to write a poem for our holiday collection, he was able to apply the use of imagery in a poem about books:

> Books
>
> A book absorbs me
> When I open it
> It sends tiny arms out
> That take me in
> A book is a dream land
> We can know
> And cannot resist
>
> It is magical
> Like a cuddly kitty
> That purrs to you

I'm not exactly sure how Adam made the leap from his incomplete raven pieces to his rich, imaginative poem about books. Partly it was a matter of time—just living and learning around other poets. I'm certain with him that having the opportunity to share his work publicly with other writers also contributed to his growing confidence and ability as a poet. However, if I had to name one thing that contributed to his growth as a poet, it was that through experience and support, Adam found his voice. He figured out a way to pull the vivid images soaring around like ravens in his mind and use his voice to express them in printed form.

With other poets who prefer to work more privately, I listen to their poems and try to point out places where their voice seems clearest. For example, Michael worked for months on a collection of short, simple poems about animals. He even devised a map for organizing the topics about which he planned to write (Figure 25). Each time he wrote one I pointed out the strength of the poem, encouraging him to keep writing. Growth happened in small increments, and celebrations were not shared with others, at Michael's request. In time, after his voice became more confident, he wrote a wonderful poem about horses and cowboys (Figure 26). He finally found the courage to write clearly, honestly, and in a way that was beautifully descriptive. With that poem Michael became a true poet.

Figure 25

We have to stay with emerging poets who are just discovering their voices. Whether it happens as a process of privately highlighting what they are doing well, or focusing publicly on strengths and accomplishments, we need to remain close to them and their work until their voices are strong. Every poet's voice develops differently and in its own time. A big part of our job as teachers of young poets is to allow for those differences in our classrooms.

Horses and Cowboys

As the sun comes up
early
all the horses are
awake

As the cowboys come out
all the horses are
ready
for a run in the fields

They run through
the swift wind
they go

–Michael

Figure 26

One important difference to consider is that not all poets have serious voices, and those who do aren't necessarily serious all of the time. Indra, who wrote the lovely poem in the front of the book, spent many writing periods playing around with words. She delighted in using her writing voice to make others laugh. Her poem "Cattle Drive" (Figure 27) was one of her greatest triumphs as far as humor is concerned. She was more than pleased with herself for her ability to use puns and surprising twists to keep her audience chuckling. Her voice reminded us all that we don't always need to take life so seriously, that sometimes it's all right to just have fun.

Cattle Drive

Cowboys drive
cattle in a car and
drive them crazy and
weird and wacky

The cowboys drive the
cattle to the train
and the train drives
the cattle even more
crazy and wild and wacky
and weird...

–Indra

Figure 27

Donald Murray (1987) writes, "We must teach ourselves to recognize our own voice. We want to write in a way that is natural for us, that grows out of the way we think, the way we see, the way we care" (184). With some young writers the process of finding their voice involves helping them discover what they passionately care about and then putting that passion into words. Mikey played around with several poems about his new puppy (Figure 28) before settling on one called "Little Warm Bud" (Figure 29). With each poem he explored different aspects of his relationship with his new dog, each time trying out the voice he wanted to use that most closely

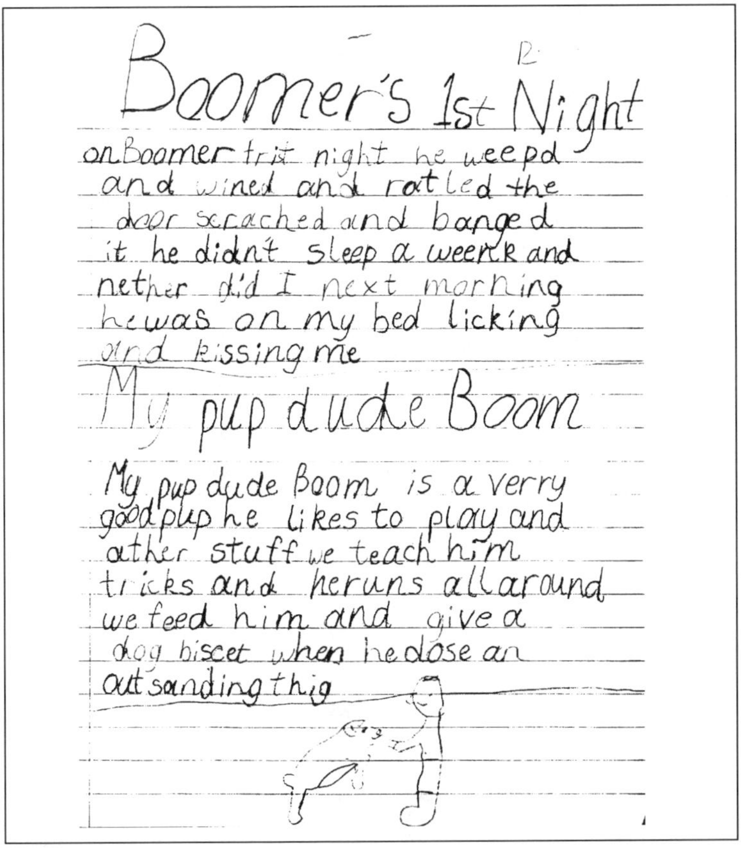

> **Boomer's 1st Night**
>
> on Boomer frit night he weepd
> and wined and ratled the
> door scrached and banged
> it he didnt sleep a weerk and
> nether did I next morning
> he was on my bed licking
> and kissing me
>
> **My pup dude Boom**
>
> My pup dude Boom is a verry
> good pup he likes to play and
> ather stuff we teach him
> tricks and he runs all around
> we feed him and give a
> dog biscet when he dose an
> out sanding thig

Figure 28

expressed how he felt. I encouraged him to keep exploring the same topic, since his puppy was foremost in his mind. I was happy to see him examining his relationship with his puppy from different angles, and he felt my support in this process. He wasn't afraid to try out several poems, to play around with words in the same way he played around with his puppy. In this process he was true to his own voice and to the love he felt for his pet. I think he selected "Little Warm Bud" because it was written with the truest voice and it most clearly captured his feelings.

Little Warm Bud

I have a little
warm bud
I cuddle him
walk him and play with him
I also call him Boomer
my little puppy dude
and he's my little warm bud

–Mikey

Figure 29

When we assist young poets in their quest to find their own voices, we are enabling them to allow the truth of their lives to come through. We are teaching them that what they have to say matters more than remaining safe and silent. In a sense, we are helping them find their way as human beings to the deeper parts of themselves.

I often tell my students that writing poetry helps me sort out and make sense of my life experiences. When I feel agitated, it often means a poem is ready to be hatched out onto the page. When the poem is written with a voice I know to be true, then I find balance once again. We talk about this in class, trying to name the process of finding one's voice. The more we talk about it, the more it begins to make sense over time. When I discover a young poet who has found his or her voice, I try to point it out, either privately or publicly. When voices are noticed in gentle ways, they become stronger.

When we help children find their voices as poets, we empower them to tap into their inner courage. Many times children face difficult situations that are out of their control, and certainly out of ours as their teachers. When a child's family is split by divorce or when a favorite grandparent passes away, we can do little but offer moral support. Not long after Denise lost her grandmother, she began the process of sorting out the experience and remembering her "Too-Too." She wrote this short poem one day:

> I once had a grandmom
> who was good she warmed
> hearts and when my mom had coffee
> she didn't have cream so
> my grandmom was the cream in
> her coffee

We can't remove the troubles in our students' lives, but we can help them find their voices so that they can begin to express what is in their hearts and eventually make sense of it all. We can't give them answers, but we can lead them down a path where their writers' voices may help them discover answers on their own.

In addition to revealing insights into our own lives when we find our writer's voice, we can help others find theirs. When we hear another writer's words describing a life event or feeling, those words often resonate for other poets also. Upon hearing a poem written by one child, another might think, "I have felt that way," or "I could write about that, too." When we find our voice as a poet and share it with others, they, too, may be inspired to work a little harder or let down their guard a bit more to write the truth of their heart. When others hear the truth of one heart, they begin to see that something more is happening than just words on a page. Many of them will want to experience it themselves. This happened in my class recently after Jenna read a poem she wrote about her friend Emily, who transferred to another school (see Figure 30).

After Jenna read her poem, we proceeded with our quiet writing time. Poets seriously entered their thoughts in their daybooks. When I made my daily rounds to check in with

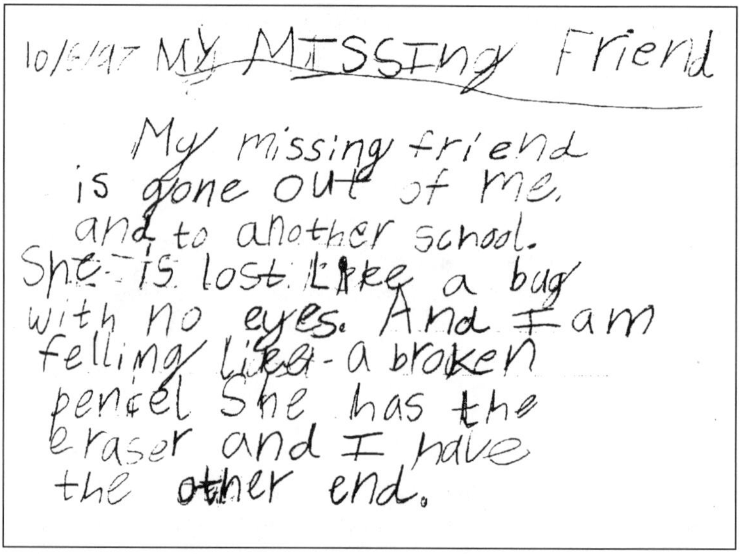
10/6/97 My Missing Friend

My missing friend
is gone out of me.
and to another school.
She is lost like a bug
with no eyes. And I am
felling like a broken
pencel She has the
eraser and I have
the other end.

Figure 30

each child, I was surprised to find two poems, one by Sydney and the other by Indra (see Figures 31 and 32). It's hard to know exactly what inspires this kind of poetry in children. Certainly the love they feel for a friend contributes to what they write. But I also believe that seeing and hearing how another child has found her voice, and used it to write in a profound way about what matters to her, elevates the level of writing young poets produce. Jenna's voice helped others find theirs.

This idea may seem too advanced for young children to think about. Yet children have a way of knowing truth subconsciously. They know when a poet has found his or her voice and respond accordingly. If poetry has voice, it will hold their attention and they will want to hear more. They will also be inspired to write more in ways that are deeply moving and complex beyond what we ever dreamed they could do.

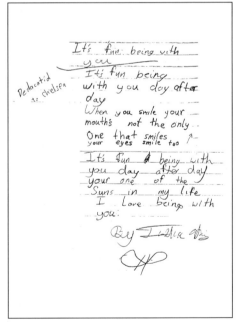

the hosing home.
the home of
OLD and Yog.
I Prsah is so spashto
me to me she Falt
Like the moon
and I was the
litta Star.

BY Sydney

The Nursing Home
The home of old and young.
One person is so special to
me. to me she felt
like the moon
and I was the
little star.

Dedocatid
to Chelsea

It's fun being with
you
It's fun being
with you day after
day
When you smile your
mouths not the only
One that smiles
your eyes smile too

It's fun being with
you day after day
your one of the
Suns in my life
I Love being with
you.

Figures 31 & 32

CHAPTER SEVEN

A Swarm of Bees

When we returned to school after Spring Break, some of the girls noticed bees burrowing in the mud walls on Tasha's property. Jesse announced, "Trouble for the Tashameister!" This made Chelsea a bit nervous, so she moved her mud bowl to another spot. Almost instantly, Teagan, Mikey, and Jesse formed the Bee Patrol. Their enthusiasm was overwhelming, and not necessarily appreciated equally by everyone. When Indra noticed them near her property and heard Teagan announce, "We're going to open up the World of Bees!" (as if it were going to be an amusement park), she said, "Heh, scientists. Ask me before you invade my house!" Paying little attention to Indra's request, the Bee Patrol continued their quest to investigate the bees:

Mikey: We need to dig out holes to get them to move out. We're
      digging to see how protective they are.
Jesse: See if they come out and try to sting.
Mikey: If they do it'll be really hard to get them to move.
Teagan: Do you want some scientists to live with you?
Tasha: You can live in my house as long as you live in this garden,
      but don't move them out.
Mikey: If you don't, you'll get stinged. If we bug their house really
      bad they'll come out.
Teagan: Maybe the queen bee'll come out.
Mikey: We have to get the workers out. Without the workers, the
      queen will starve.

90

Jesse: If he comes at us we know he cares.
Teagan: Heh, he's got pollen on him! You know we had to make up
      pretend food, now we can have real food!
Jesse: We're never going to learn anything if we're not brave!

Later when we returned to the classroom, Teagan's passion for
investigating the bees was verified in her log entry (Figure 33). This
passion continued in the weeks that followed as the Bee Patrol
developed theories, constructed special goggles for viewing the bees,

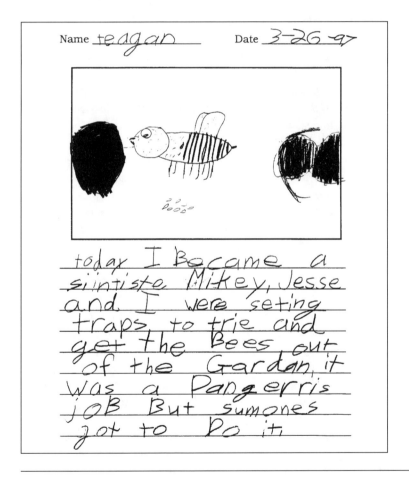

Name teagan   Date 3-26-97

today I Became a
siintiste. Mikey, Jesse
and I were seting
traps, to trie and
get the Bees out
of the Gardan, it
was a Dangerris
joB But sumones
got to Do it,

Figure 33

and tried out various scientific tests to see how protective the bees were. At all times they remained curious but respectful of the bees, our cohabitants in the garden. One day they observed that the bees were spreading out. Jesse announced, "The bees are spreading out. There's a different group like in Sim Ant. Red ants vs. black ants. Maybe they fight each other in the garden." Later he solicited donations: "Donations! Donations for the Bee Patrol!" When Sean got too close to the bees, Jesse exclaimed, "Sean, move! There's a bee hovering around in his attack mode! It's hovering with its back to us!" Teagan, Mikey, and Erik came over to watch it come out of the hole. One of them commented, "We were right. They're spreading out! When it leaves we're going to plug that hole."

    As our spring days passed by and the end of school loomed ahead of us, I was thinking one morning that I needed to find a metaphor to describe this group of children. I considered several— ants, desert flowers, garden plants, butterflies emerging from cocoons. In the midst of my reverie, the Bee Patrol brought my attention to a swarm of bees that had gathered on a bush just outside the fence. Mikey explained, "They're making a hive but it's not a hive yet. You just see bees. Normally you see a hive. Probably there's a little hole to get in and out, to do the honey."

    Throughout the morning children kept coming up to me asking, "Mary, did you see the bees?" It suddenly dawned on me that we had been like a hive of bees all year, busily attending to our various tasks and responsibilities to keep the colony running smoothly. Just as I was settling calmly into this appropriate meta- phor, half of the class started running into the building screaming, "The bees are out! The bees are out!" Our bees, it turned out, had a change of mind and decided to form their hive somewhere else. Through some collective understanding, they made the decision to depart instantly. Mikey shouted, "See, I told you!" Kinley added, "I guess they didn't want this beehive." Erik wasn't so sure that they were leaving for good. He said, "I think they started their colony and just left to get stuff!" Keith summarized the whole event by declaring, "It's an exciting movie!" Later in his garden log (Figure 34), Keith was more matter-of-fact in his account of the swarm of bees who gathered to carry out their work together, and then departed for whatever called them next in life.

When you begin to live your life as a poet, you can't help but see life in terms of metaphor. As a teacher of young poets, I find metaphors in just about everything that happens at school. Often it is a matter of just waiting for the right one to surface, such as the day the bees swarmed, carried out their work, and then vanished. Developing an awareness of metaphors begins as a process of opening our eyes and learning to see in a new way. Later on it translates into learning to write in a new way.

Figure 34

The work our class did in the garden was a metaphor for everything else in our school lives. The bees offered a parallel view of how we interacted together, working industriously to carry out important jobs. The mud was our poetry, shaped and reshaped into forms that expressed what was in our hearts and minds. Sometimes we just played around with it, and other times we seriously crafted it into meaningful structures. The carpet squares, shells, stones, and seeds were the inspirations from daily living that kept us writing and wanting to be poets. The Bee Patrol was a relentless reminder to always keep our eyes open, examining what is before us.

In my classroom I usually don't introduce the idea of metaphor right away; I try to give my students time to become acquainted with other aspects of poetry first. Embedded in experience with line breaks, rhyming, moods, and different poetic styles, metaphor always manages to surface at some point. Usually a discussion of simile happens at the same time.

I have found that young poets can most readily understand metaphor when it is compared with simile. I simply tell them that simile is when a poet says one thing is *like* something else. Metaphor is when the writer says a thing *is* something else, and usually the two are not literally similar. It is especially helpful to show good examples of metaphor at this point.

A very short poem with a strong, clear metaphor is "When It Is Snowing" by Siv Cedering (Janeczko 116):

When It Is Snowing

When it is snowing
the blue jay
is the only piece of
sky
in my
backyard.

I also include poems written by other children to demonstrate simile and metaphor. Daniel's poem (Figure 35) is an excellent example of the use of simile and one that has enabled many of my young students to understand simile. Andréa's

"Life Is a Poem" (Figure 36) is especially appropriate for this lesson because she uses both metaphor and simile, making it easy to see the difference.

Once we begin talking about simile and metaphor, the children notice how other poets use these elements of poetry. In a sense, they begin to develop a new way to see poetry and a new way to see their world. As with all aspects of school, different children apply their understanding in unique ways. Many children don't move beyond simile when they're just beginning their journey as poets. They make connections between various experiences and tie them together by saying that one thing is like another. And then there are other children who seem to have a natural sense of how metaphor works. These children become important teachers for all of us. Jesse is one of those teachers.

How A Poem Is Like

A poem
    is like
        a cloud
the bumps
    are like
        the words
the clear part
    is like the
        rhyming
the raindrops and snow
    are like
        the ink
and the sky
    is like
        the pen

--Daniel

Figure 35

On the day Jesse shared the first draft of his poem "The Feel of Them" (see Figure 12, page 57), I asked him if he was finished with it. He thought for a moment and then said, "It's still hatching." This comment opened up a class discussion of how poetry comes to us if we put ourselves in a position to receive it. Poetry also appears if we are patient enough to wait for it to hatch. On this day the energy and concentration in the class were almost tangible. Children were making connections like I'd never seen before. I asked if anyone noticed what was happening. Many of them were able to comment on their improved abilities as poets. As our discussion began to wind down, I asked the children to write out their thoughts about what had just occurred. This was Jesse's response, written in about five minutes:

LIFE IS A POEM

Life is a poem with
Flowers that have just
Had a new birth
The wind is like the
Voice of the sea
A shell upon the water's edge.
The breeze makes
the boats flow the
sea is blown
with the wind by
my side I feel
as though I am with
the wind all the time
I feel I do everything
with the wind.
I can tell the wind
my lifetime stories.
If I lived by the
beach, I would visit
the beach every day.

Andréa

Figure 36

Poem Poets

We are hatching
great poems from
our circular minds
our circular minds are
laying more poems
every miraculous moment
of our heart pounding
life

Once again, he amazed me with his natural ability to use metaphor. With a minimal introduction to the idea of metaphor, he applied it in ways many adults are unable to do after years of practice. That day Jesse taught me an important lesson. He showed me that a good poetry program will produce results if children are given time and a vast amount of experience with all kinds of poetry. He demonstrated the kind of writing and thinking that are possible when we assume our students are capable of exceptional work. Jesse reminded me that, as teachers, we can give our students a new window through which to see the world by introducing them to ideas such as metaphor, even when they are very young. And finally, he taught me that when these concepts are presented to young poets in appropriate ways and when the poets are given opportunities to keep practicing what they know, the concepts will remain with the children as they mature both as writers and as human beings.

Just recently, Jesse and I sat together talking about poetry. He was trying to think of ideas for poems by making a list of topics. He settled on a poem about his soccer team, the Sun Sharks. As he wrote I could almost see the metaphors filtering into his mind. He wrote "ball" and then immediately crossed it out and replaced it with "spotted circle." This was his first draft:

Sun of the Sharks

The spotted circle
flies up
one
foot follows

the foot
kicks it far
and
high the
ball bounces
off the
feathers
of a goalie
it is a goal
people cheer

I asked him about the use of the word "feathers" in the line "the ball bounces off the feathers of a goalie." He said that he'd been thinking of birds and how the hands of a human reminded him of the bone structure of a bird's wing. I then asked him to write down a few thoughts about this specific idea (see Figure 37 for what he wrote). I asked him to explain about the eagle. As he held out his hand to explain the similarity between the eagle's finger bones and the human hand bone, he said, "Actually, it's not the feathers that are similar. It's the talons." Before I could respond, he crossed out the word *feathers* and replaced it with *talons.* We both agreed that *talons* made more sense in the context of the poem and he felt satisfied with what he'd written.

Jesse's story is an important one for several reasons. It shows, first of all, what is possible with young poets if they receive the proper training. It is true that Jesse's writing is exceptional for an eight-year-old, and most of his peers will not reach this level of understanding metaphor for many years to come. Yet he demonstrates the kind of writing that can be done by a young poet when his senses are made aware of an

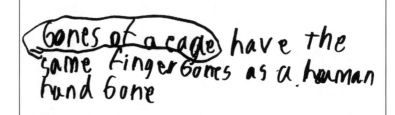

Figure 37

alternative way to process and explain the world. As a member of the bee patrol, Jesse spent a considerable amount of time squatting down near the mud wall where the bees had burrowed. He waited, watched, made predictions, developed theories, and continually attempted to find new ways to explain what he saw. Jesse never stopped trying to make sense of what he observed. His passion for understanding the bees was not unlike his passion for explaining the world through metaphor.

Young poets like Jesse who have this kind of passion for metaphor can teach us a great deal. Some are helpful with peers by being good listeners, by asking questions, by offering suggestions to other poets. In Jesse's case, he was most profoundly a teacher when he sat in the author's chair and read his lines of surprising metaphor. He showed us what is possible by not being afraid to occasionally take a poetic leap and put words together in unusual ways. He, and others like him, open up windows of possibility for themselves each time they write and share their work—and they allow us to make the journey with them when we have the opportunity to hear and see what they've written.

Each time I read another one of Jesse's poems, I find myself asking the question: How does he do it? Every opportunity to work with Jesse on his writing is a new mini-lesson for me. I learn as much as he does. Once again we are on equal ground, both teaching and learning from each other.

Jesse's story is valuable because it offers hope. Hope that a new generation of writers is growing up seeing the world with a slightly different view. Young poets like Jesse will continue to approach their lives and their writing in much the same way that they approached the bees—carefully observing, developing personal interpretations, and then actively going about the business of letting others know what they have seen. Jesse and his generation of new poets will not be afraid to look closely at what passionately interests them. Nor will they be intimidated by the potential sting of failure, for they know that their metaphors carry important messages that the rest of the world needs to hear—messages that will pollinate the lives of poets for years to come.

CHAPTER EIGHT

Under the Palo Verde Tree

Spring in Arizona is a glorious season. Unlike in colder climates when the grip of winter is finally released, spring in the desert is a last fling before facing months of relentless summer heat. It's a time of celebration, especially for everyone in the garden after nearly a year of learning and living together.

Over a period of a few weeks, Denise and Tasha (with help from Teagan and Caitlin) organized the Mad Rock Performance Group. They began by making tickets for their show and rehearsing original songs such as "I Love My Kitty" and "I Don't Like the Doctor." One afternoon they gathered their first audience near the storage shed in the shade of the huge palo verde tree—the same tree that provided the seeds for our garden economy.

The audience was surprisingly attentive and impressed with the girls' first song. I asked if they'd written it themselves or if they heard it somewhere else. Denise said they'd written it themselves and then announced their next number: "I Don't Like the Doctor." She added, "If you don't have a ticket or if you're poor you can come for free. Do you want 'I Love the Doctor' or 'I Don't Like the Doctor'?" Indra, who was sitting nearby, asked, "How about 'I Hate the Doctor'?" Denise quickly replied, "You can't use that word!" (I had requested that the word hate not be used in the garden or our classroom.) After they finished their song I asked, "But what if we didn't have doctors?" Denise said, "We don't like the medicine!" Then they sang "I Love the Doctor." The show continued:

Denise: Raise your hand if you want us to sing "I Don't Like the

Orthodontist" or "I Don't Like the Nursery."
[The kids in the audience raised their hands for the one they wanted.]
Mona [my teaching assistant]: What's the deal about the nursery?
Erik: It's where you buy plants and stuff.
Denise: Natasha has to go there when her mom goes to the gym!
Mikey: I have to go there, too.

Soon after "I Don't Like the Nursery" was performed, most of the audience dispersed. Throughout the remainder of the afternoon I could hear lines from "I Love the Doctor" sung in various corners of the garden. The Mad Rock Performance Group had made their mark.

The following week they were on stage again, this time to perform an original rap song written by Denise. Inspired by our recent study of the Civil Rights Movement and the connections she'd made with her own African American heritage, Denise had composed this song about Rosa Parks:

> One day Rosa Parks
> Was riding a bus
> And they said
> Get up and give it away
>
> Give, give, give
> It away.
> Now Rosa Parks said
> No, no, no way.
>
> Give, give, give
> It away.
>
> Now they said black
> Lady you're going to jail
>
> Give, give, give
> It away.
>
> Now that lady
> Banged on those
> Rails for days and days.
>
> Give, give, give
> It away.
>
> Until one fine day
> A hero came his name
> Was MLK he said no
> more of this stingy stuff so

Give, give, give
It away.

The content of Denise's song was exceptional and her delivery was even better. As she tossed her braids about, singing of her hero Rosa Parks, the whole audience was captivated. She played handmade instruments, and even pulled Teagan from the crowd to join the stage show. At the audience's request they sang the song about Rosa one more time. In the protective shade of the palo verde tree, a songwriter was born—and celebrated by an audience that knew a star was among them.

I realized the day Denise performed her Rosa Parks song that our work in the garden and our work as poets had finally intersected. Like Kinley and Bryan's miniature adobe blocks that cured in the sun, our months of dabbling in mud and metaphor had taken on a form that could be used for self-expression and celebrated by those fortunate enough to witness both the process and product. The Mad Rock Performers brought their talents as writers to the stage where they knew their work would be well received. They knew, perhaps, that there were others among them who would recognize their passion for sharing poetry in motion and applaud their efforts. They were ready to go public with what they had created.

Most of what we do in class to further our work as poets focuses on process. Our writing is in a continual state of emergence, each line somehow leading us to the next one. Our discussions, mini-lessons, and daily writing practice are all part of this journey to perfect our craft as poets. We pause to hear each other's lines or the lines of well-known poets, and then continue with our writing. We are on a mission to unearth the lines of our lives.

The Mad Rock Performers confirmed the value of process. They revealed what delightful music and entertainment can happen when children are given the time and opportunity to play with an idea and develop it. They also reminded me how important it is to include moments of celebration as part of the process. Celebration is essential for many reasons:

◆ It is a time to honor the wonderful works children have produced.

◆ It helps inspire other poets to stretch themselves, to go beyond their current developmental level as writers.

◆ It is an opportunity to learn from each other and see new possibilities for topics, styles, techniques, and forms.

◆ It is a way to publicly acknowledge the importance of poetry writing for both personal development and for the benefit of others.

◆ It is a time to pause and appreciate how truly remarkable it is that young poets are able to do what they do so well.

In our daily classroom life we incorporate celebration in a number of ways. The most frequent and basic form of celebration occurs during author sharing. At the end of each writing period, or sometimes at the beginning, one or more child reads her or his work to the class. The author of the day sits in a designated chair and others gather around on the floor. He or she reads the selected poem. I often ask for the poem to be read a second or third time, to hear the lines more completely. We listen for lines that surprise us or stand out as exceptional. We attune our ears to the presenting poet's voice and try to respond in ways that will further his or her development as a writer. Children make comments and offer suggestions:

◆ How did you get the idea for that poem?

◆ I liked how you used simile to compare those two things.

◆ You used really interesting description in that one line.

◆ What were you feeling when you thought of the last line?

◆ Your poem reminded me of the time . . .

◆ I liked your poem a lot and it seems like it needs another verse—I want to hear more.

◆ That's one of the best poems I've ever heard.

The poet who has shared leaves the author chair knowing his or her work has been appreciated. Even if suggestions for improvement are made, the poet feels encouraged and supported by fellow writers. This simple forum for sharing work serves as a mini-celebration for daily work and plays a significant part in the continuation of inspired writing.

Poetry is also celebrated in our classroom by displaying it on the walls. I mentioned earlier that each week I select a poem (or song) for a child which goes into our class anthology. I also ask the children to draw a self-portrait which I mount on construction paper with the child's name and poem to hang on the wall. As the weeks of school accumulate, so do the poems and self-portraits. It's a wonderful way to celebrate the class as well as the poetry dedicated to each child.

The children's poems are also displayed on the wall. As early in the year as possible, I begin typing their poems and hanging them on the classroom walls. Once the children see their classmates' poetry displayed, they want others to view theirs as well. For example, when Andréa wrote a poem about her father, we quickly made it available for others to see. Not long after that, Denise wrote a poem about Harriet Tubman (Figure 38) and wanted it exhibited beside Andréa's.

Poetry can and should be celebrated across the curriculum. Just as we read literature and nonfiction books in our pursuit of studies in science and the social sciences, we can also include poetry as part of the learning process. Poems that teach us information, such as those mentioned in Chapter 5, can be another means of teaching content. In addition to poems by published poets, I always try to include content-related poems written by classroom authors. For example, while we are studying the Underground Railroad, a poem like Denise's (see Figure 38) about Harriet Tubman can easily be incorporated into lessons and displays of pictures and other materials. Keith's poem (Figure 39) would be a wonderful addition to a study of space. When we use poetry to celebrate what we know in all areas of the curriculum, it reinforces the idea that poetry is important in all areas of our everyday lives, too.

I use poetry to celebrate learning in another way. Occasionally I will ask my students to write a poem in response to a study, specific experience, or learning event. Although my intention is not to use the poem as an assessment tool, a poem written as a culmination experience often reveals much about a child's learning. Denise's poem about Harriet Tubman demonstrates her knowledge of Harriet's strong spirit, efforts to help free other slaves, and words of inspiration. Reading

Figure 38

our students' poems written in response to school studies gives us a private opportunity as teachers to celebrate all of the wonderful learning they have experienced. And some poems, like Indra's "The Evening" from a surprise end-of-the-year collection, leave us with much to ponder about the impact of our work on young lives:

> The Evening
>
> The sky
> is filled with beautiful colors
>   that glow,
> but why?
> We may never know.
>
> The colors flow
> like a river
> but we regret when they go.

Indra's poem is about the sky, and perhaps that is all she was thinking of when she wrote it. But it is also about the end of something, an end full of beauty and celebration, and also regret that what has been will no longer be. Indra's poem is about the year ending, and a tribute itself to a significant chapter of her life. As a teacher, reading a poem like Indra's makes all efforts worthwhile.

Sometimes finished poems end up in other classrooms. Particularly if another class is studying a related topic, or if a child wants a former teacher to see his or her progress as a poet, we make sure a special poem is shared. It is not unusual in our school for both younger and older children to share their work with other classes. A child may even be asked to participate in a mini-lesson to teach others about a new poetry discovery. In addition to sharing the poem, the child might describe his or her process and answer questions from other students. In this way, celebration helps to teach as well as honor.

Our school has two publications in which poetry is often celebrated. We have a biweekly newsletter that features a quote of the week from a child. At times a poem is included in this section, such as Anita's poem about the wind (Figure

40). We also publish *The Seed News,* an annual newspaper produced by the second graders, which includes school news, staff interviews, recipes, sports summaries, and poetry (Figure 41). The poetry of a five-year-old might be printed alongside that of a nine-year-old, with all lines acknowledged in the same way.

Within our classroom we publish poetry collections around themes or in response to specific studies. One year we published a collection of Halloween poems called *Halloween Shivers.* In February we sometimes write love poems to give to

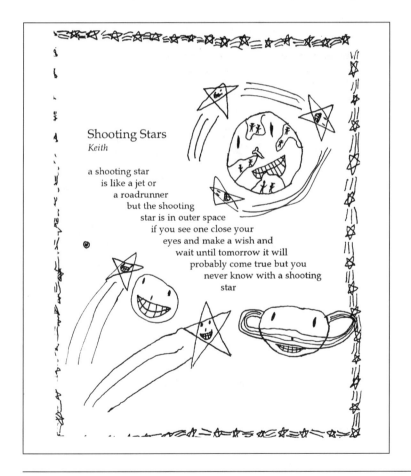

Figure 39

someone we love. Each December we assemble a collection of poems as a holiday gift for parents. This group of poems is usually varied and not specific to the holiday season. It might include a poem like Chelsea's about her favorite doll (Figure 42), along with silly poems, reflective poems, or even a poem about poetry, such as Dylan's (Figure 43). Each child makes a black-line illustration of his or her poem and then we duplicate the collection for everyone. For this collection the children make hand-painted covers, and we spend extra time

THE SEED NEWSLETTER

1130 W. 23rd Street • Tempe, Arizona 85282-1810   (602) 829-1479

Read-a-thon
We're still in the process of adding up totals for the Seed Read-a-thon. Results will be available next week. Please be sure to remind sponsors to send in their pledged amounts as soon as possible. Thanks to Jan Muchow and Maria Wong for their work on this year's Read-a-thon.

Birthday Party
Mark your calendar for April 13th! It's the Seed's 20th birthday celebration. Invitations were distributed in mailboxes last week and if you didn't receive one, please let Patricia know. If you know of anyone who went to the Seed but didn't receive one, please have them call 829-1479 and we'll send an invitation. We're still in the process of updating our mailing list.

Registration for Fall and Summer '97
Registration for fall and summer begins today. We advise you to enroll your child as early as possible, especially for summer school. If you have any questions, please see Mary or Patricia.

Friday Holiday
There is a Friday holiday this week (see the Seed Calendar) and no classes will be held. The regular schedule resumes on Monday, March 31st.

CLASS NEWS
Kerri/Sandi/Shelley
3's and Young 4's
Earthworms and spring flowers are popping up around the classroom. Before break we had a discussion on worms and discovered many facts that we already knew about the wiggly things. A shipment of live earthworms should be arriving in the next few days. We're planning to create a class compost pile and adopt a few to take home by Earth Day

to cultivate the gardens in our own backyards. Thanks to Rita Jo Anthony, Joseph's mom, for sharing her expertise on seeds. She helped us prepare and sow native Blue Palo Verde seeds, Arizona's state tree. We hope the seedling will be ready for transplanting soon. Our Spanish color books are almost ready--we're finishing covers this week.

Mike/Connie
4's and Young 5's
We have made it to the letter R in our alphabet books, and S in our art projects. In addition to wrapping up our alphabet study, we will spend the next couple of weeks preparing something to be auctioned at the school picnic in April. Literature and projects related to the season will also be featured, as well as author sharing.

Kathy/Tim
PreK-Kindergarten
A tidal wave of enthusiasm for the ocean has engulfed our class as we have initiated studies, shared materials and

QUOTE OF
THE WEEK

_____

The Wind Is
Calling Me

The wind is calling me.
The wind is calling me.
  One time, two times.
The wind tells the trees
  and the trees tell the
  branches.
  Tell the leaves,
    tell the wind,
  that I am here.
The wind tells me
  and I hear.

--Anita Lin, age seven

March 24, 1997   The Seed Newsletter

Figure 40

binding each book so it will be a durable addition to their permanent libraries at home.

As I mentioned earlier, we also produce a similar collection at the end of a study. I have collections in our classroom library written in response to our visits to the nursing home, desert studies, and a study of Native Americans. Over the years our class has often written poetry in response to the human rights study we do annually. Stefanie's poem "Slave Girl" (Figure 44) is an example of the kind of poetry included in this type of collection.

The Seed News — Page Fifteen

POETRY

Love the Earth
Dawn Franco

Please don't litter,
Love the earth.
Don't smoke at all,
That pollutes.
Please take care of the earth.
Throw things in the trash cans.
I love the earth and the earth loves me.

What Is That Up There?
Jenna Hoppe

I look at my desert
What do I see?
I see the sky up in the air.
There is the moon and the stars
and the sun peeking out from the mountains.
There is something hiding up there.
But what is hiding way up there?
Up from the ground, what could it be?
I think I see it.
It is a cloud hiding.
All the other clouds are calling
"Come with us, you are covering the sun
up there."
And that is just what the
cloud did.

MY BUCKER
Cam Bay

My Bucker is hard to describe
He's not an ordinary dog
He has a golden color
    to his skin
He is a very quiet type
He's got a soothing pat
He considers himself
    as a Golden Retriever
He strolls through the yard
    with his balls
He only barks
    in his certain way

    Bucker

Sirens
Sean Maddox

Sirens sing on rocks.
People hear the songs.
It's so beautiful to be true.
They daydream from the wonderful songs.
They sing and sing until the full moon
shines on them.
Then they return to their home.
They come every day to sing.
The people sing with them, but they still
don't know who sings.

In My Garden
Allison Cripe

In my garden I can see a rose
in front of me.
A tulip as well as a rose could be
for my friend, with love and care
in my garden.

THE INVINCIBLE
David Buckingham

When she falls down in soccer
She always gets up
When she gets kicked
She keeps on going
She is a woman of steel
She never gives up

When she had a very bad disease
She kept on fighting
And she beat it
She is the best sister
In the whole world
Now you know
Who she is
She is my sister
And I love her

THE UNSUSPECTED
Nick Autrey

On that dry ice I have the puck
When suddenly Kaboom!
I am on the ground
My legs bent
One on the left

One on the right
I am hopeless to get up
And nobody understands
That I am hurting
They just sit on the bleachers
Staring at the puck
While inside the mask
There is pain
Most of them haven't played
The aggressive game of hockey

Hockey is life to me
I have played it a long time
Myself getting injured
On that hard ice
My brother checking me on the street
Without pads most times
But now
God gives me courage
And I fight back

LITTLE SANTA AND THE VERY LITTLE ELF
Christopher Fierro

It was the night before Christmas
What's this I see?
A little Santa and his very little elf
Standing by my tree

Figure 41

Poetry is celebrated in other ways besides the class anthologies. A growing number of young poets I work with manage to fill pages and pages of their daybooks with poetry. Both Oliver and Andréa published an end-of-the-year collection of poems they believed were their best. It gave them a chance to select not only their favorites, but also to review and celebrate in a private way the fine body of work they'd generated over the year.

On occasion, poetry from our class finds other audiences with whom we can celebrate. One year we practiced and performed a collection of pig poems for our friends at the nursing home. Included among the nursery rhymes and poetry by published poets was Susan's "A Piggy Wiggy's Pen" (Figure 45), a take-off from the book *Piggy in the Puddle* by Charlotte Pomerantz (1974). Susan was delighted that her poem was used for a public performance, and her classmates equally enjoyed the process, knowing that the work of someone they knew and cared about was receiving the recognition it deserved.

Figures 42 & 43

Unlike with Susan's poem when the celebration is planned, poetry in our classroom is sometimes honored without any effort or intention on our part. These situations may appear insignificant and are often missed if we're not paying attention. One example of this is a note Jenna's mom wrote on her weekly homework sheet after Jenna wrote the poem about her friend Emily (see Figure 30, page 88). Her mother simply wrote, "I liked Jenna's poem about Emily and the broken pencil—did you?" Her recognition of Jenna's fine writing, as well as her effort to communicate how pleased she

Figure 44

was with her daughter's poem, was a subtle, yet powerful message that she celebrated the young poet in her family.

Another example of this kind of quiet, unplanned celebration is when visitors come to our class. As teachers we spend so much time with a group of blossoming poets, it's easy to lose sight of how truly remarkable their work is. We grow used to the powerful metaphors and unusual lines they write each day. When visitors come and read their words displayed on the wall or in collections on bookshelves, they are often taken aback by the power of the writing. Recently a

A Piggy Wiggy's Pen
by Susan

a piggy wiggy pig plays in a puddle
piggy wiggy
          piggy wiggy
plays in the puddle all day
along with a splash

pig in the middle of the puddle with a
          COME IN, MY FRIENDS
now there are eight piggies
in the middle of the puddle

they call their friends
now there are eighteen piggies
in the middle
          of the puddle

now there are more piggies
in the piggy wiggy puddle
and they all are having
          a piggy wiggy good time
and this piggy poem ends
with the piggies
          calling more friends saying

THE END

Figure 45

woman was visiting our school to find out more about how the curriculum works. After giving her a tour of the entire school, we ended up in my classroom. I explained the various aspects of our daily schedule, some of the studies we'd conducted, and described a few of the projects in which we were involved. As the tour neared its completion, I pointed out a poem that had just been added to the wall collection. Our visitor read it and turned to me with tears in her eyes. Without saying anything, she told me in that moment that she understood what our school was about and in her own heart celebrated the children's fine efforts in their writing and other work. By making poetry available for others to read, the children's lines have the potential to influence many lives in profound and important ways. Readers like this sensitive visitor are changed by the children's poetry, and in turn meet the world with just a slightly different perspective, having been touched by their words.

In addition to the many kinds of celebration that occur in our classroom regarding poetry, there is one remaining way in which it can be used. When a class has reached its final days together, poetry is an excellent way to bring closure to the experience. When we reached our last few weeks of school, we ventured out to the garden one afternoon, this time with our daybooks in hand. The days were warming up by then, so everyone scrambled to select the most comfortable shady place they could find, mostly in the shelter of the palo verde tree. There was no one who needed help getting started— everyone had something to say. Tasha wrote about the voices she heard under the tree and the perfume and paint she'd made. Indra used a simile when she wrote "It's like a houseful of Nature and all kinds of creatures." Mikey addressed the noise and commotion along with the peace, love, and friendship that grew in our garden. Kelly mentioned "the polite bee patrol." Bryan, the boy who earlier in the year sat staring at a blank page for two weeks before writing a poem, ended his with "in the garden/you can do all sorts/of fun things like/ making adobe bricks/and sitting writing poems/on a tree."

Eventually the poems were typed, illustrated, and assembled into a collection called *Out Here*. Each child also received an end-of-the-year award with his or her poem and a photograph from the garden on it. As the awards were handed out with parents looking on, there was a story that accompanied each child's poem and photograph. The poetry and stories revealed the profound impact of this experience on all of our lives.

On our last day outside, we dismantled everything. Bricks, tiles, stones, pieces of wood, shells, and other materi-

Garden

The seeds, like many dotted treasures
The sand, like millions of rocky dots
The glass water jars, like little
bowls of water that won't
evaporate
The church, like a place
of celebration
The garden, a place
of celebration and fun!

--Erik

- 20 -

Figure 46

als were sorted out into piles along the fence. I gave each child a baby food jar in which to collect a few small items to remember the garden. Most put a small adobe block and some seeds in their jars, as well as other significant artifacts. After we finished this bittersweet task, we stood around under the palo verde tree and I asked if anyone had anything to say. Everyone was quiet for a few moments and then Erik spoke up: "I'm feeling really sad right now. I don't want the garden to end. It seems like we just got started."

Erik's poem from the collection (Figure 46) doesn't reveal his sadness about the year coming to an end. Perhaps when he wrote it, the full impact of the year's end hadn't sunk in. What it does express is his attention to the details that made the experience so meaningful. His poem moves from "the glass water jars, like little/bowls of water that won't/evaporate" to an understanding of the larger meaning of the experience. Erik's poem captured what a celebration our few hours each week in the garden had been for all of us and served as a reminder that, like the jars of water that wouldn't evaporate, the memories of our days as poets and comrades in the shade of the palo verde tree would remain for a long, long time.

CHAPTER NINE

In Honor of
the Butterfly

In late October Oliver spotted a dead butterfly underneath a curved tile. It was in near-perfect condition. He exclaimed, "A butterfly! It's a huge one. It's dead!" Dylan wanted to put it in a jar. Bryan rushed over and gently held it in his hand. Other children soon joined the growing circle of curious onlookers and wondered what kind it was. Oliver announced, "We're going to make a grave for the butterfly." I suggested he wait until we found out what kind of butterfly it was and so everyone could see it. He said, "We're going to bury it after they see it."

After Oliver finished searching reference books and surveying the class to document opinions about the butterfly, we decided on a day for the "ceremony." We assembled near his space by the fence. At first Oliver was a bit overwhelmed and didn't know what to say. Rather than burying the butterfly, he placed it in a clear plastic box so it could be seen. He had a ceramic dish for money which he planned to put by the butterfly's grave when people came "to greet it" and he said, "If you're really poor you can take some." Once Oliver explained his plan for the butterfly, I suggested others might want to say something about the butterfly:

Teagan: The butterfly must have been very beautiful when it was
    alive.
Tasha: I think it died of its old age.
Indra: I think it lived a happy life and it died peacefully.
Anita: I think it died of old age and its wing.
Michael: Something got its wing.
Teagan: I wish it was still alive.

After a few words were said, some of the children put a few seeds and rocks on the dish. I asked if they wanted to sing a song. Some wanted "By and By" and others wanted "Simple Gifts," so we voted right in the middle of the ceremony. It was about half and *half, so we ended up singing both. After the songs I asked if there was anything else we needed to do. Oliver said we should pray. In order to respect various religious backgrounds, I suggested we have a moment of silence so everyone could pray in their own way. Then Oliver placed the butterfly in its plastic container underneath a bush by the side of the building.*

In the months that followed, Oliver developed the area near the butterfly grave into a "church." He brought sweet peas from home to plant and organized a little altar around the casket. At one point Oliver made a cross and placed it in the church. As I watched him prepare this quiet space in the midst of our bustling community, I couldn't help thinking of him as some sort of holy man, assigned to the humble task of preserving the sacred in a world almost too busy to notice it.

For a while Oliver just worked quietly by himself, but soon the church grew into a bigger operation. Sarah, Leigh, and Anita joined him and took over an old school desk they called the "church desk." They spent weeks arranging and rearranging natural objects on the desk, putting mud on it and then washing it off, and establishing a place where visitors could sign up to go to the church. Sarah brought a sage bundle (often burned by various Native American people for purification) and hung it from a nearby bush. They put shells on the desk and tapped them to make sounds. Sarah and Leigh gathered up some old cow bones lying around the garden and hung the spine off the edge of the desk. One vertebra became a pencil holder. They used the rib cage and one loose rib as a xylophone, which they placed near the butterfly grave. As they worked Sarah said, "It could be an instrument." Anita added, "Or part of a dead cow."

Although the church group was one of the most sustained and active groups, most of the children involved seemed to lack a clear concept of what "church" is. They knew that something sacred was involved, and singing. But beyond that it appeared to be a great deal of circling around what the idea of church might be. One day Denise dropped in on the church and took them to task on this: "Where's the preacher? Where's the seats? Where's the Bible? Where's the snack bar? Where's the bathroom?"

Sarah replied, "It's not a regular church." The amount of ambiguity that surrounded the church was amazing to me. It was equally fascinating to observe how they changed their talk about the church to meet the various challenges others presented to them.

When someone questioned their practices or ideas, they just revised their story.

Another interesting feature was the wishing well Oliver and Sean made adjacent to the church. It consisted of a plastic container inside another container. Players threw a seed in the container, and if it landed in the middle one, they could scoop up a handful of seeds and make a wish. If their wish didn't come true they received some other sort of prize. Other games developed. One variation was a game where each player had to answer a math problem. Anyone who came up with the correct answer was given a prize and a chance to make a wish.

The wishing well and other games became popular garden pastimes. Unfortunately for the adobe builders, the wishing well drew crowds that were boisterous and distracting. After a long discussion in class about zoning, we came up with a plan to move the wishing well to a less populated area. Everyone was up for it except Oliver.

The day he finally agreed to move it, there was a disagreement with another child over where it should be set up. Oliver became upset about this and cried inconsolably. At one point I noticed him hiding behind a bush, looking like he was trying to make himself invisible. Teagan approached Oliver and tried to talk to him but he wouldn't come out. I decided to go over to the church desk and have a little talk with the girls. I discreetly pointed out Oliver behind the bush. Anita said, "Maybe we could surprise him!"

They went right to work on it. Teagan approached me and said, "Mary, here's your job: Distract him for ten minutes." Kelly and I invited Oliver to accompany us to the tool storage room to find a pair of hedge trimmers. When we returned outside, a mob greeted Oliver with a surprise. They had fixed up the wishing well for him and he was delighted. Teagan summarized the experience in her garden log:

Today Oliver was feeling bad so we cheered him up by setting the wishing well up while Mary kept him away and he seemed like he didn't like it at first but after awhile he loved it and everybody liked it. They came over and it seemed like the line went all the way to the ball park. We have a lot of money but we had a lot of fun! That is one thing I'll never forget is the way the church saved the day and why.

And Oliver wrote:

Today I got a surprise. It was the wishing well. Teagan helped me make it look better when I was away. And I want to say a big thanks to the people who made the wishing well beautifuller.

In time Oliver shifted to other work. He and Anita busied themselves stirring a huge clay pot of mud, making Chinese fireworks "without gunpowder." He walked around collecting sticks and organized them into little arrangements. He made flower perfume and devoted his days to making the garden a more beautiful place. Through his persistent activity, Oliver quietly reminded us to hold sacred the part of ourselves wherein beauty and truth reside.

As I reflect on our year in the garden, the "church" remains at the forefront of my thoughts, not for any particular religious reason, but because of what I believe it represented within our community. Observations of Oliver and the "church desk" workers helped me make important connections between our work in the garden and the classroom. The church emerged as a powerful metaphor for what happened through our daily efforts as poets.

Like the church, poetry writing with young children is a constant state of revision. It grows and changes in response to whatever enters our lives. As we gain experience, the writing we produce becomes more refined and closer to the truth of who we are. The resilience of poetry allows for this constant change, just as the church workers were able to change their story when others questioned their thinking or actions.

Writing with young poets can be an excellent outlet for trying to answer the hard questions we face in the process of living. I say "we" because as teachers, we have the opportunity to learn as much as our students. We learn from what they write and what we ourselves write alongside them. Poetry writing is a way to sort out what is hard to know, an attempt to put words to something that is difficult or takes a long time to understand. In a sense, poetry helps us make order in our lives. Much like Oliver, who established the shrine to the deceased butterfly, our poetry writing helps us honor what we recognize is important but full of unanswered questions. Oliver's quest to understand wasn't limited to the garden—he spent the remainder of the year writing poems about angels. At times playful and other times more serious, he stayed with his fascination of what is beyond physical life as we know it.

The level of activity surrounding the church desk was a strong reminder of our need as writers to have a community, a place to be social and to belong. The children's continual support of each other (e.g., the day the wishing well was moved) and collaborative efforts to sort out the meaning of things carried them much further than if they'd been working alone. As I look around the classroom during silent writing, this sense of belonging is strong and clear. I see writers who care about what they're trying to say and writers who care about each other. I am not surprised when Mona, my teaching assistant, approaches me nearly as eager as the children, asking to share this poem:

> My hands are aging before my eyes
> The nails are getting ridges
> And the skin is full of lines
> My veins are near the surface
> Bumpy and greenish blue.
> Little lumps are forming on a few
>   of the joints
> Sometimes I rub them—
> They still do work
> And they get chapped this time of year
> I am thankful to have them.

As poets we all know we are part of a greater community of writers who have come and gone through the ages. Just recently we met a elderly man named John at the nursing home. He was new to the facility and eager to tell his life story. Amid details about having been a fifth-grade teacher, a principal, a superintendent, and college professor, he mentioned that he was a published poet. After a long and full life, he is still thinking and talking about poetry. He said, "I still think it's one of the best ways to get your feelings out." When I repeated his story to the class, I could see a recognition in many of the children's eyes that our community of poets had just increased by one. They felt excited for John because they knew why poetry was important to him.

In addition to being an attempt to answer the unanswerable or a place to belong, the church in our garden was a reminder to hold sacred and honor those who have come before us. The butterfly was not human, but it was a beautiful life-form that existed and passed on before we arrived. Oliver's shrine to it was a place to remember the beauty of who and what we love. Poetry in our classroom functions in much the same way. Andréa's poem about her father is an appreciative tribute to the deep ties of love she feels for him:

A Real Dad

a real dad takes you fishing
a real dad
would love you
he would talk
about his love
for you before you were born
if you want to know how I know
it is because I have that
kind of dad

The collection we assembled around Valentine's Day extended this idea to include parents, pets, stuffed animals, siblings, and other significant influences in our lives. Through writing about those we love, we give honor to that which has brought us to this point.

Writing poetry also allows us to practice who and what we want to be. We can try on different feelings and responses within the safety of our own daybooks. We can feel secure in sharing what we are exploring as writers because we know we are surrounded by others doing the same. Like the church desk workers who were in a perpetual state of transformation—both in their physical arranging of the desk, as well as the rearrangement of their stories—we have the flexibility as writers to change what we think and how we want to respond to life's experiences. When we write we find out who we are and, I believe, come to know the deeper and higher aspects of ourselves. In other words, poetry becomes a way of knowing. Classrooms where this kind of work is encouraged become places where the participants have a better chance to reach their potential as writers and as human beings. As this process occurs, children, teachers, and classrooms are transformed, much like the butterfly held sacred in Oliver's church.

The church in our garden was most definitely a place where symbols were stored. The butterfly was an obvious one and there were others—the bones, the sage bundle, and the cross. I doubt that when the children placed an object there they consciously thought, "I'm putting this here as a symbol of _____ ." Yet, in their own young ways of knowing, they recognized the importance of each object and made sure it had a place among other sacred artifacts. One of the most significant symbols within the context of the garden was the wishing well.

I don't believe it was by chance that the wishing well was attached to the church. The boisterous activity it generated was anything but church-like, yet it made perfect sense that it was included. The wishing well was an opportunity for participants to try to make their dreams come true. It was a chance to make a connection between what is and what could be. So it is with poetry.

When we give children the time and space to develop as poets, we offer them that same sense of possibility. Poetry won't necessarily make their wishes and dreams come true, but it does allow them to consider many more options than if they'd never written. Through our work with young poets, we can open up the world to them. In turn, they give us back their fresh and unique ways of seeing and knowing.

Our year in the garden is over and a new group of children has claimed the space. There are no baby food jars of colored water this year, and the butterfly has long since crumbled and turned to dust. But the palo verde seeds remain a solid indicator of a healthy economy, and adobe block production continues. Most of the children moved on to the next teacher, although I was able to keep seven of the children for another year, this time as third graders. Oliver and Denise are two of the children who have remained to carry on the previous year's garden traditions. There have been changes, however.

Recently I was surprised when Denise proclaimed that Oliver had turned over the church desk to her. I asked what she was planning to do with the desk, and she replied, "It's going to be the front desk of the kids' mall." One day as she organized her wares and the crowd of potential buyers hovering around the desk, I had to chuckle (knowing I was at the same time writing this book about poetry) when she announced, "Everyone, form a line! Form a line!"

As poets we are still forming our lines. Jesse is no longer in my class, but we meet every two weeks just to check in and talk about writing. He is using poetry to process his feelings about his dog Bud, who is suffering from a terminal illness. Oliver continues to write angel poems, and just the other day Erik spontaneously wrote a poem and then rewrote it with line breaks. Like the palo verde seed economy, our work as poets is thriving.

Although these young poets are strong and committed to writing, there is an element of vulnerability that cannot be ignored. Just a few days ago when we were out in the garden, I asked Oliver if he was thinking of reopening the church. "Maybe," he said, "but the church is dead." I asked him why he thought it was dead. He said, "Because it's a mall now." I suggested, "Couldn't you have the church without the church desk?" He replied, "But there's no place to write." His words reminded me that our single most important job as teachers of young poets is to ensure that they will always have a place to write. If we can provide that place and make available what knowledge we have, they will know what to do from there. The sacred space we make for them to write the poetry of their lives will bear fruit as wondrous as a garden—a garden rich with the soil of possibility where wishes and dreams can come true.

The Garden

The garden holds all my
feelings, the way a book holds a
story. The garden holds all my
secrets. The rocks hold everything
that I heard. The wind holds the
story of me and the garden.
Every plant tells the love and care
I used on it. But what matters
most to me in the garden are my
friends.

—Jenna, age 8

References

Chawla, Louise. 1994. *In the First Country of Places: Nature, Poetry, and Childhood Memory.* Albany, NY: State University of New York Press.

Fletcher, Ralph. 1993. *What a Writer Needs.* Portsmouth, NH: Heinemann.

Graves, Donald H. 1983. *Writing: Teachers & Children at Work.* Portsmouth, NH: Heinemann.

Heard, Georgia. 1992. *Creatures of Earth, Sea, and Sky.* Honesdale, PA: Boyds Mills Press.

———. 1989. *For the Good of the Earth and Sun: Teaching Poetry.* Portsmouth, NH: Heinemann.

———. 1995. *Writing toward Home: Tales and Lessons to Find Your Way.* Portsmouth, NH: Heinemann.

Heidegger, Martin. 1971. *Poetry, Language, Thought.* Trans. Albert Hofstadter. New York: Harper & Row.

Janeczko, Paul B. 1990. *The Place My Words Are Looking For.* New York: Bradbury.

Kennedy, X. J., and Dorothy M. Kennedy. 1982. *Knock at a Star: A Child's Introduction to Poetry.* Boston: Little, Brown.

Livingston, Myra Cohn. 1994. *Animal, Vegetable, Mineral: Poems about Small Things.* New York: HarperCollins.

Lyne, Sandford. 1996. *Ten-Second Rainshowers: Poems by Young People.* New York: Simon & Schuster.

Murray, Donald. 1989. *Expecting the Unexpected: Teaching Myself and Others to Read and Write.* Portsmouth, NH: Heinemann.

———. 1987. *Write to Learn.* New York: Holt, Rinehart & Winston.

Norris, Kathleen. 1996. *The Cloister Walk.* New York: Riverhead Books.

Nye, Naomi Shihab. 1992. *This Same Sky: A Collection of Poems from Around the World.* New York: Aladdin Paperbacks.

———. 1995. *The Tree Is Older than You Are: A Bilingual Gathering of Poems and Stories from Mexico with Paintings by Mexican Artists.* New York: Simon & Schuster.

Oliver, Mary. 1994. *A Poetry Handbook.* New York: Harcourt Brace.

Pomerantz, Charlotte. 1974. *The Piggy in the Puddle.* New York: Simon & Schuster.

Prelutsky, Jack. 1984. *The New Kid on the Block.* New York: Greenwillow.

Rilke, Rainer Maria. 1949. *The Notebooks of Malte Laurids Brigge.* New York: Norton.

Tenzin Gyatso, Dalai Lama XIV. 1990. *The Good Heart.* Trans. Geshe Thupten Jimpa. Boston: Wisdom Publications.

Recommended Works

* collections I use most frequently

General Children's Poetry Books

Carle, Eric. 1989. *Animals, Animals.* New York: Scholastic.

Chandra, Deborah. 1988. *Balloons and Other Poems.* New York: HarperCollins.

Clarke, Gillian. 1996. *The Whispering Room: Haunted Poems.* New York: Kingfisher.

*Cullinan, Bernice E. 1996. *A Jar of Tiny Stars: Poems by NCTE Award-Winning Poets.* Honesdale, PA: Boyds Mills Press.

dePaola, Tomie. 1988. *Tomie dePaola's Book of Poems.* New York: Putnam.

Fleischman, Paul. 1988. *Joyful Noise: Poems for Two Voices.* New York: Trumpet.

Fletcher, Ralph. 1991. *Water Planet.* Paramus, NJ: Arrowhead Books.

Florian, Douglas. 1994. *Bing Bang Boing.* New York: Harcourt Brace.

Frost, Robert. 1959. *You Come Too: Favorite Poems for Young Readers.* New York: Henry Holt.

*Goldstein, Bobbye S. 1992. *Inner Chimes: Poems on Poetry.* Honesdale, PA: Boyds Mills Press.

Graves, Donald. 1996. *Baseball, Snakes, and Summer Squash: Poems about Growing Up.* Honesdale, PA: Boyds Mills Press.

Harwayne, Shelley, ed. 1995. *Jewels: Children's Play Rhymes.* Greenvale, NY: Mondo.

*Heard, Georgia. 1992. *Creatures of Earth, Sea, and Sky.* Honesdale, PA: Boyds Mills Press.

Hoberman, Mary Ann. 1991. *Fathers, Mothers, Sisters, Brothers.* New York: Scholastic.

Hopkins, Lee Bennett. 1990. *Good Books, Good Times!* New York: Trumpet.

———, ed. 1994. *Hand in Hand: An American History through Poetry.* New York: Simon & Schuster.

———. 1983. *The Sky Is Full of Song.* New York: Harper & Row.

*Janeczko, Paul, ed. 1990. *The Place My Words Are Looking For.* New York: Bradbury Press.

Kennedy, X. J., and Dorothy M. Kennedy, ed. 1982. *Knock at a Star: A Child's Introduction to Poetry.* Boston: Little, Brown.

*———. 1992. *Talking Like the Rain.* New York: Little, Brown.

Koch, Kenneth, and Kate Farrell. 1985. *Talking to the Sun: An Illustrated Anthology of Poems for Young People.* New York: Henry Holt.

*Livingston, Myra Cohn. 1994. *Animal, Vegetable, Mineral: Poems about Small Things.* New York: HarperCollins.

———. 1992. *I Never Told and Other Poems.* New York: McElderry Books.

*Lyne, Sandford, ed. 1996. *Ten-Second Rainshowers*. New York: Simon & Schuster.

O'Neill, Mary. 1961. *Hailstones and Halibut Bones*. New York: Trumpet.

*Panzer, Nora, ed. 1994. *Celebrate America in Poetry and Art*. New York: Hyperion Books.

Prelutsky, Jack. 1984. *The New Kid on the Block*. New York: Greenwillow.

———. 1994. *A Pizza the Size of the Sun*. New York: Scholastic.

———. 1986. *Read-Aloud Rhymes for the Very Young*. New York: Knopf.

———. 1986. *Ride a Purple Pelican*. New York: Greenwillow.

———. 1990. *Something BIG Has Been Here*. New York: Greenwillow.

———. 1988. *Tyrannosaurus Was a Beast*. New York: Scholastic.

de Regniers, Beatrice Schenk, Eva Moore, Mary Michaels White, and Jan Carr, eds. 1988. *Sing a Song of Popcorn*. New York: Scholastic.

Reid, Barbara. 1987. *Sing a Song of Mother Goose*. New York: Scholastic.

Ridlon, Marci. 1969. *Sun through the Window: Poems for Children*. Honesdale, PA: Boyds Mills Press.

Rogasky, Barbara. 1994. *Winter Poems*. New York: Scholastic.

Silverstein, Shel. 1996. *Falling Up*. New York: HarperCollins.

———. 1981. *A Light in the Attic*. New York: HarperCollins.

———. 1974. *Where the Sidewalk Ends*. New York: Harper & Row.

*Sullivan, Charles, ed. 1989. *Imaginary Gardens: American Poetry and Art for Young People*. New York: Abrams.

Whitman, Walt. 1988. *Voyages*. Edited by Lee Bennett Hopkins. New York: Harcourt Brace Jovanovich.

*Yolen, Jane. 1987. *The Three Bears Rhyme Book*. New York: Harcourt Brace Jovanovich.

———. 1995. *The Three Bears Holiday Rhyme Book*. New York: Scholastic.

Bilingual/Multicultural Poetry Books for Children

Begay, Shonto. 1995. *Navajo Visions and Voices across the Mesa*. New York: Scholastic.

Delacre, Lulu. 1989. *Arroz con Leche: Popular Songs and Rhymes from Latin America*. New York: Scholastic.

*Giovanni, Nikki. 1971. *Spin a Soft Black Song*. New York: Farrar, Straus and Giroux.

*Greenfield, Eloise. 1986. *Honey, I Love and Other Love Poems*. New York: HarperCollins.

Griego, Margot C., Betsy L. Bucks, Sharon S. Gilbert, and Laurel H. Kimball, eds. 1981. *Tortillitas Para Mama and Other Nursery Rhymes*. New York: Henry Holt.

Hudson, Wade, ed. 1993. *Pass It On: African-American Poetry for Children*. New York: Scholastic.

*Hughes, Langston. 1994. *The Dream Keeper and Other Poems*. New York: Knopf.

Lomatewama, Ramson. 1993. *Drifting through Ancestor Dreams*. Flagstaff, AZ: Northland Press.

———. 1983. *Silent Winds: Poetry of One Hopi*. Hotevilla, AZ: Ramson Lomatewama.

Mitchell, Adrian. 1989. *Strawberry Drums*. New York: Delacorte Press.

Mora, Pat, ed. 1996. *Confetti: Poems for Children*. New York: Lee and Low Books.

*Nye, Naomi Shihab, ed. 1992. *This Same Sky: A Collection of Poems from Around the World*. New York: Aladdin.

*————. 1995. *The Tree Is Older than You Are: A Bilingual Gathering of Poems and Stories from Mexico with Paintings by Mexican Artists*. New York: Simon & Schuster.

Orozco, José-Luis, ed. 1994. *De Colores and Other Latin-American Folk Songs for Children*. New York: Dutton.

Philip, Neil, ed. 1996. *Earth Always Endures: Native American Poems*. New York: Viking.

Pomerantz, Charlotte. 1980. *The Tamarindo Puppy and Other Poems*. New York: Greenwillow.

Sneve, Virginia Driving Hawk, ed. 1989. *Dancing Teepees: Poems of American Indian Youth*. New York: Holiday House.

*Sullivan, Charles, ed. 1991. *Children of Promise: African-American Literature and Art for Young People*. New York: Abrams.

————. 1994. *Here Is My Kingdom: Hispanic-American Literature and Art for Young People*. New York: Abrams.

Music for Inspiring Poetry Writing

African Voices: Songs of Life. 1996. Milwaukee, WI: Narada. Compact disc.

Bernstein, Margaret. 1992. *Full Circle*. Santa Rosa, CA: Growing Azalea Music. Compact disc.

Coyote Oldman. 1990. *Thunder Chord*. San Francisco: Hearts of Space Records. Compact disc.

Deep Forest. 1992. New York: 555 Music/epic. Compact disc.

Eaton, William. 1994. *Where Rivers Meet.* Phoenix, AZ: Canyon Records. Compact disc.

Enya. 1991. *Shepherd Moons.* New York: Reprise Records. Compact disc.

Handel, George Frederic. 1978. *The Water Music.* The Academy of Ancient Music. London: Decca Record Co., Ltd. Compact disc.

Liebert, Ottmar. 1990. *Nouveau Flamenco.* Los Angeles: Higher Octave Music. Compact disc.

Master of Classical Music series: Vivaldi, Mozart, Bach. 1988. Los Angeles: Delta Music. Compact disc.

Nakai, R. Carlos, and William Eaton. 1988. *Carry the Gift.* Phoenix, AZ: Canyon Records. Compact disc.

Sanctuary: 20 Years of Windham Hill. 1996. Stanford, CA: Windham Hill Records. Compact disc.

Winston, George. 1994. *Forest.* Stanford, CA: Windham Hill Records. Compact disc.

Poetry for Grown-up Readers

Clifton, Lucille. 1987. *Good Woman: Poems and a Memoir 1969–1980.* Brockport, NY: BOA Editions, Ltd.

Dickinson, Emily. 1990. *Selected Poems.* New York: Dover.

Dove, Rita. 1993. *Selected Poems.* New York: Vintage.

Hughes, Langston. 1959. *Selected Poems of Langston Hughes.* New York: Vintage Books.

Kenyon, Jane. 1993. *Constance.* St. Paul, MN: Graywolf Press.

Neruda, Pablo. 1988. *Late and Posthumous Poems: 1968–1974.* Trans. Ben Belitt. New York: Grove Press.

————. 1988. *The Sea and the Bells.* Translated by William O'Daly. Port Townsend, WA: Copper Canyon Press.

Nhat Hanh, Thich. 1993. *Call Me by My True Names.* Berkeley, CA: Parallax Press.

Norris, Kathleen. 1995. *Little Girls in Church.* Pittsburgh: University of Pittsburgh Press.

Nye, Naomi Shihab. 1995. *Words under the Words.* Portland, OR: Eighth Mountain Press.

Nye, Naomi Shihab, and Paul B. Janeczko, eds. 1996. *I Feel a Little Jumpy around You: Paired Poems by Men and Women.* New York: Simon & Schuster.

Olds, Sharon. 1990. *The Dead and the Living.* New York: Knopf.

————. 1992. *The Father.* New York: Knopf.

————. 1992. *The Gold Cell.* New York: Knopf.

————. 1996. *The Wellspring.* New York: Knopf.

Oliver, Mary. 1990. *House of Light.* Boston: Beacon.

————. 1992. *New and Selected Poems.* Boston: Beacon.

————. 1991. *White Pine.* New York: Harcourt Brace and Company.

Pastan, Linda. 1991. *Heroes in Disguise.* New York: Norton.

Rilke, Rainer Maria. 1989. *The Selected Poems of Rainer Maria Rilke.* New York: Vintage.

Ríos, Alberto. 1988. *Lime Orchard Woman.* Riverdale-on-Hudson, NY: Sheep Meadow Press.

————. 1990. *Teodoro Luna's Two Kisses.* New York: Norton.

Savard, Jeannine. 1988. *Snow Water Cove.* Salt Lake City, UT: University of Utah Press.

————. 1993. *Trumpeter.* Pittsburgh: Carnegie-Mellon Press.

Trungpa, Chögyam. 1983. *First Thought, Best Thought.* Boulder, CO: Shambala.

Walker, Alice. 1991. *Her Blue Body Everything We Know.* New York: Harcourt Brace Jovanovich.

Author

Mary Kenner Glover has lived and worked in Arizona since the early 1970s. Seeking an alternative educational setting for her two young daughters, Mary co-founded Awakening Seed School in Tempe, Arizona, in 1977, where she is currently the director and second-grade teacher. She completed her master of arts degree in elementary education at Arizona State University in 1988. She has authored *Making School by Hand, Charlie's Ticket to Literacy, Two Years: A Teacher's Memoir,* and co-authored *Not on Your Own: The Power of Learning Together.* In addition to her work as a teacher and educational consultant, Glover is a poet and an artist. She lives in Tempe, Arizona, with her husband and youngest daughter.

This book was typeset in Optima and Goudy Heavyface
by Electronic Imaging.
The typefaces used on the cover were Futura, Helvetica,
Arquitectura, Garamond, AGaramond, and Benguait.
The book was printed by Versa Press.